MARITAL MYTHS
REVISITED

Marital Myths

Revisited

*A Fresh Look at
Two Dozen
Mistaken Beliefs
About Marriage*

Dr. Arnold A. Lazarus

Impact Publishers,® Inc.
ATASCADERO, CALIFORNIA

ATTENTION ORGANIZATIONS AND CORPORATIONS:
This book is available at quantity discounts on bulk purchases for educational, business, or sales promotional use. For further information, please contact Impact Publishers, P.O. Box 6016, Atascadero, CA 93423-6016, Phone: 1-800-246-7228, e-mail: sales@impactpublishers.com

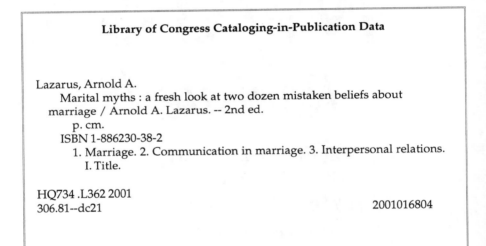

Library of Congress Cataloging-in-Publication Data

Lazarus, Arnold A.
    Marital myths : a fresh look at two dozen mistaken beliefs about marriage / Arnold A. Lazarus. -- 2nd ed.
        p. cm.
    ISBN 1-886230-38-2
        1. Marriage. 2. Communication in marriage. 3. Interpersonal relations.
        I. Title.

HQ734 .L362 2001
306.81--dc21   2001016804

Publisher's Note
This publication is designed to provide accurate and authoritative information in regard to the subject matter covered. It is sold with the understanding that the publisher is not engaged in rendering psychological, legal, financial, or other professional services. If expert assistance or counseling is needed, the services of a competent professional should be sought.

Impact Publishers and colophon are registered trademarks of Impact Publishers, Inc.

Cover design by George Foster, Foster & Foster, Inc. Fairfield, Iowa
Printed in the United States of America on acid-free paper,
Published by *Impact* 🕊 *Publishers®, Inc.*
POST OFFICE BOX 6016
ATASCADERO, CALIFORNIA 93423-6016
www.impactpublishers.com

C O N T E N T S

PREFACE

*I*n the years that have ensued since the publication of *Marital Myths* in 1985, I have treated hundreds of additional couples, attended numerous workshops, seminars and professional meetings on couples therapy, participated on several educational panels, and read many new (and some old) books and articles on marriage and couples therapy. Given this additional information, it seemed worthwhile to revisit *Marital Myths* to determine where I would now disagree with or still adhere to the views expressed therein.

A colleague, in reference to a book he had published in 1949, said that he would change nothing whatsoever in it — not even a comma. I found this astounding. Surely the passage of time yields new information, additional data, and sheds light on hitherto obscure points of view? Some experts contend that virtually everything is out-dated by the time it gets published.

I hope that the readers of *Marital Myths Revisited* will find value in considering the points that seem to have stood the test of time, and those that now seem dated or faulty and need to be corrected. Learning from someone else's mistakes, misconceptions, and revised thinking should be a useful way of gleaning helpful information. At the end of each commentary, a list of essential conclusions will enable the reader to zero in on the most helpful directives with minimal time and effort.

INTRODUCTION

A marriage license, unlike most other licenses, is not granted on the basis of competence. The holder of a license to practice medicine has demonstrated some knowledge of body ills and cures; a driver's license implies that the person has shown at least minimum competence behind the wheel of a car. If high schools routinely offered courses in "marriage competence," much as they do "driver education," it is likely that more people would know how to develop sensible, workable, and loving nuptial agreements. The question is, who would be qualified to teach these courses? Many marriage counselors, psychologists, psychiatrists, and other mental health practitioners labor under as many false conceptions as the clients they counsel or treat. Most people don't know how to be married!

Most couples enter marriage with impossible dreams and unrealistic expectations. Whatever else marriage connotes, it is essentially a partnership and an occupation. For some it is a full-time vocation. If people wrote out *job descriptions*, fully listing exactly what they wished to give and get from marriage, and if each potential partner studied the other's lists *before* getting engaged, much grief and many dashed hopes could be averted.

Let me pose a hypothetical situation. John and Mary, in their early twenties, have been going together for two years and are intent on marrying each other. Here is John's job description:

I expect a wife to be a loyal, loving, devoted companion. I want someone who really studies my needs and caters to them. As I see it, a husband should be at the center of his wife's universe. Nobody and nothing should come before her husband. One main reason for marrying is to have someone taking care of all my creature comforts — I do not expect to do any cooking, cleaning, shopping, and so forth. I expect a wife to work at remaining sexually attractive, responsive, and desirable. I would want sex at least once a night. I expect my wife to treat my parents and my sister with the same love and respect that I do. As I see it, the duty of a wife is to build up her husband's ego and self-confidence. At the same time, I feel that the man should be the captain of the ship, he should be the boss, and he should be consulted before the wife makes any important decisions.

Independently, Mary prepares her job description:

Marriage is teamwork, and it consists of two people who are equal partners pulling in the same direction. There should be more "ours" than "his" or "hers." Married people should function as responsible adults, with little mothering or fathering of each other. They should set up their own home and become independent as soon as possible and not lean emotionally on parents or siblings. I would want to be sure that I come first in my husband's eyes. I expect to have help around the house with routine things — we would clean house together, go food shopping together, and operate as a team.

Given even these very brief and general "job descriptions," I think it is obvious that if John and Mary got married, they would soon run into conflict. You might ask how they could have spent two years in close proximity without discovering such obvious differences of style and opinion. In truth I have treated hundreds of married couples who came face to face with widely differing expectations and flagrant incompatibilities only after living together, despite prolonged courtships in some instances. In today's world, where most people tend to live together before marriage, obvious clash points sometimes come to light in time to save the situation. But this is not inevitable. I have worked with many couples who lived together, subsequently married and only then discovered insurmountable differences that had not emerged earlier.

When counseling couples premaritally, I routinely use the "job description" method. Some people have trouble spelling out their expectations; they cannot articulate precisely what they hope to contribute to and derive from marriage. It is the therapist's job to help that person ferret out exactly what he or she is hoping for. The marital job description is a useful device in such cases, achieving exactly the same thing as typical job descriptions in the work situation. "In this job," says the personnel manager, "we expect you to do A, B, and C." The job applicant can decide whether the salary is in keeping with the demands, if that sort of work is appealing and whether or not he or she is qualified. When would-be marriage partners spell out their "A, B, and C" requirements and expectations, the same decisions can be reached — is the payoff sufficient, does the liaison seem to have sufficient fun, enjoyment, and compatibility built into it, and is the person able to give and take the necessary emotional material to sustain it?

I have been practicing marriage therapy, sex therapy, and psychotherapy for over forty years. It has been my habit to watch other professionals in my field very closely. Many have been kind enough to allow me to sit in and observe them with their patients or clients. (As I grew more experienced, I too allowed students and colleagues to observe me in action.) This is perhaps the best way to learn what to do and what not to do. As I think back to the way I handled (or mishandled) some of the couples who had consulted me when I first got started, I shudder a little! Practice doesn't make perfect, but it does enable one to iron out many of the bugs!

The idea for this book grew out of the reactions that have typically been evoked whenever I have spoken to groups on the subject of marriage relationships. I have lectured on treatment techniques, research methods and findings, with audience response ranging from boredom to enthusiasm, but whenever the topic of *marital myths* was introduced, there was invariably an intense interest. Everyone considers himself or herself an expert on the subject, and very strong opinions predominate. When I discuss one or more of the myths in this book, people are eager to take sides — those who agree with me form one camp; those who disagree form another, and the sparks fly!

When treating couples, I usually ask them to identify specific myths to which they adhere, and often type out a short list of do's and don'ts for them to work on between sessions. The results are invariably enlightening to them, and often highly emotional.

If you wish to inject some life into a boring party, a dull book club meeting, or any other group of people, you might try bringing up the subject matter of this book!

My points of emphasis throughout this material are grounded in Western, English-speaking cultures. In different areas of the world, the game of marriage is played by entirely different rules. What works well in Seattle might be a disaster in Singapore! This is not a book that can be translated into many different languages and sold world-wide.

I selected the two dozen myths that form the basis of this book from my own case studies, rereading notes I had taken during sessions, listening to cassette recordings of couples I had treated. The twenty-four myths that emerged are the most prevalent I found in my practice (although they are not presented in order of importance). There are many others (some of which are alluded to in the book) but I consider this collection to represent the most common mistaken beliefs that result in marital dissatisfaction.

All the people referred to in this book are drawn from actual case histories. Names and other identifying characteristics have been altered to maintain confidentiality.

COMMENTARY

It is abundantly clear that the *expectations* (both overt and covert) that people bring to their marriages will have a most profound effect. More often than not, regardless of the specific complaints a couple may present, the underlying theme is "this relationship is not providing me with what I had hoped for or expected." Sometimes, these expectations turn out to be unfair or unrealistic, and therapy can provide a course correction. Quite often, each partner's expectations seem fair and fitting, but they had not been spelled out or clearly articulated. Couples contemplating marriage are strongly advised to share exactly what they expect of one another. If you are already married and things are not going too well, commence by clearly thinking about and then discussing your expectations in as direct and open a manner as possible.

Despite my proclamation that this book is geared to Western cultures and would not be applicable in different regions, it has been translated into many languages including Spanish, Portuguese, German, Italian, Chinese, Swiss, and Dutch. Perhaps marriage has more continuities and similarities among different nationalities than I had realized. Even among my Indian friends whose marriages are typically arranged by senior family members, expectations play a key role. For example, in one young Indian couple, problems arose from the fact that whereas the husband held traditional values (he expected his wife to play a subservient role), the young lady, who had spent several years in England before their marriage, embraced more egalitarian expectations. The husband's father (a psychiatrist) sent them to me for counseling and we managed to work out an acceptable compromise.

To reiterate. If you are contemplating marriage, consider and spell out your respective expectations as lucidly as possible. If you are married or in a committed relationship, discuss each of your joint and individual expectations with a view to eliminating or modifying those that are problematic, and ensuring that the rest will be mutually fulfilled.

MYTH 1

Husbands and Wives Should be Best Friends

 Many people contend that marriage is a relationship that carries the principle of friendship to its ultimate and most intimate degree. I think they are mistaken.

The structure of marriage overlaps with friendship but is not synonymous with it. Marriage is *intimate sharing,* whereas friendship is *shared intimacy.* Friends typically do not live under the same roof year in and year out. As such, their shared intimacies are intensive, rather than extensive. Spouses share many daily events in which the feeling tone of one partner has a direct effect upon the other. Consequently, it is easy to overload the system. Moreover, friendship emphasizes the needs and interests of two independent people, while the focus of marriage usually ends up being on the family.

The meaning of having a "best friend" is intriguing. Children and adolescents often single out a particular person whom they call their "best friend." In some adult circles, the idea is viewed as juvenile. Mature and "sophisticated" adults who sneer at the idea of cultivating a best friend may have many so-called "close friends." Often these friends are no more than nodding acquaintances, work associates, or even competitors or antagonists. In truth, relatively few people are capable of establishing a best friend.

Genuine friendship presupposes a climate in which all feelings and emotions are given ample freedom of expression. There is consistent and unfettered sharing of all that is important. It is easy to know what one's best friend really thinks and feels about the significant aspects of his or her own being, and what each friend really thinks and feels about the other. This is because best friends make themselves transparent to one another; the full expression of each other's genuine thoughts and feelings is welcomed. Best friends do not feel one way and act another. They play no false roles with each other. Anger is not stifled, misdirected, or denied: it is expressed spontaneously and constructively. Sincere friendship is predicated upon a mutual desire for cooperation rather than competition. Vicarious joy is an essential ingredient — each taking pleasure in the good things which happen to the other.

Cynics will probably maintain that such relationships are impossible. Indeed, true friendships are exceedingly rare. Yet the person who does not enjoy these precious interactions with someone is emotionally impoverished and psychologically underprivileged. Wealth, status, power, prestige, fame, or achievement are no substitutes.

But does this not also describe the "ideal couple," whose marriage is a testimony to friendship and more? Thus far, what I have said about friendship can apply equally well to a loving marriage. But there is more.

A best friend is, by definition, one's most intimate confidant. The relationship includes a high degree of openness and exclusive sharing. There are no "keep off the grass" signs, no emotional taboos, no unmentionable subjects. Yet in marriage, the continuously close physical proximity and all the shared burdens and responsibilities dictate the need for some degree of emotional privacy. Whereas the ideal friendship is an A-to-Z relationship, the ideal marriage should probably proceed no further than A-to-W. Unless each partner deliberately preserves his or her individuality and ensures some degree of emotional seclusion, most marriages are likely to self-destruct.

He disagreed with my thesis and asserted that his wife was his best friend, adding that he confided in her to the nth degree. "I tell her all my woes. She knows everything about me — good, bad, or indifferent. She knows my worst doubts, fears, quirks, and petty foibles." I warned him that he was making a mistake. I was aware of his talent for self-abasement, his occasional bouts of depression, some of his innermost doubts, and other information at the X, Y or perhaps even Z-end of the range. (I knew for example, that he had sexual fantasies about his wife's older sister).

As friends, these factors had no negative impact on our relationship, but I advised him against sharing too many unsavory details with his wife. He insisted that the beauty of their marriage was that there were "no holds barred." Their marriage ended in divorce approximately three years later. I recall the look of pain and bewilderment when he confided in me that his wife had said: "I feel nothing but contempt for you!" Perhaps if I had received a *daily* diet of his self-downing, as did she, I too would have held nothing more than disdain for the man. As his friend, our shared intimacies were always seasoned with enough laughs and light-hearted moments to prevent it from turning rancid.

Two other aspects of the friendship-versus-marriage issue:

1) When imaginary problems and unfounded fears arise, instead of burdening the spouse, one can turn to a best friend. The presence of a confidant with whom to share the dilemma can minimize needless pressures on the marriage. That's what friends are for.

For example, Bill was sure that he would be laid off at work. Since he and Pam were already in debt, telling her about his fears would serve no useful purpose — it would only heighten her sense of insecurity and place undue strain on the marriage. Fortunately Bill's best friend Fred was a good listener who managed to cheer him up. Two months later, when Bill was promoted, not laid off, he and Fred had a good chuckle over his pessimistic outlook. Bill was then able to tell Pam how worried he had been that he would lose his job.

2) People who have a same-sex "best friend" can attest to the fact that there is something special about man-to-man, or woman-to-woman interactions that cannot be duplicated between members of the opposite sex. All too often, people marry and drift away from their friends. They may make new friends — usually other

couples — but this cannot be a satisfactory substitute for a one-on-one, A-to-Z relationship.

Can one have a "best friend" — not a husband or wife — of the opposite sex? This is possible but highly improbable! The many important psychological differences between men and women lead me to conclude that they can be good friends, good marriage partners, good team-mates, and good work associates. When it comes to "best friends," however, I remain very skeptical.

MYTH 1 REVISITED

The emphasis here is on not overloading one's spouse. Whether or not a person views his or her spouse as a "best friend" is not as important as being cautious to avoid burdening one's partner with certain fantasies, wishes, untoward emotions, or other information that is best kept to oneself. For example, one of my patients told his wife about several obscene sexual fantasies that served to turn him on. Had he kept these images to himself (or, if necessary, discussed them with a therapist or a confidant) all would have been well. By sharing them with his wife, she felt turned off to him — just by knowing what was going on in his head during sex. Over time, this corroded their hitherto excellent relationship and it ended in divorce.

- What is the main conclusion? There are topics that ought not to be discussed with one's spouse that one may safely share with a good friend (or even a casual friend) who knows how to keep a confidence.

Romantic Love Makes a Good Marriage

The lights dim, the curtain rises, a concealed orchestra quietly plays a languorous melody of love as a man and woman stand clasped in each other's arms watching the sun slowly sinking into an iridescent sea. They exchange vows of passionate and eternal devotion. Their commitment to each other knows no bounds. Their love will transcend such prosaic barriers as cultural dissimilarities, parental objections, money, and social position. Love and romance, the greatest of life's gifts, are theirs. They will be united and the passage of time will only intensify their romance. Eventually, they will descend the hill together, silver-haired, but no less deeply and ideally devoted than the day they were wed.

This pretty picture inspires a great number of people, young and old, in our society. In search of romantic marriage, they often end up in romantic — or not so romantic — divorce. Men and women who expect to find marriage a continuation of the ecstasy of courtship are in for an enormous disappointment. Romance thrives on barriers, frustrations, separations and delays. Remove these obstacles, replace them with the intimacy and everyday contact of married life, and the ecstatic passions fade. The thrills and chills of romance are doomed in the face of day-to-day proximity. When romance dies, the couple often feels cheated. As soon as the edge wears off, when the carefree rapture is replaced by the uninteresting routine of daily life, these unhappy ex-lovers declare the marriage bankrupt. The divorce court looms around the corner.

Marriage is not a romantic interlude; it is a practical and serious relationship. A person who has been taught to expect unlimited romance will be most bitterly disappointed when he or she fails to find it. Romantic love does not question the virtues of monogamous marriage. Its emphasis is on finding *the right* partner. Once one has met this mysteriously preordained affinity, and once some magic words are spoken before priest, minister, rabbi, or justice of the peace, lifelong bliss will be theirs. Hogwash! There is not one "Mr. or Ms. Right." Literally hundreds — perhaps thousands — of people are sufficiently compatible to enter into meaningful and happy marriages with one partner. Why then is the divorce rate so high? And why have so many people developed an unhealthy skepticism about marriage? I dare say a major reason is the large number of people in our society who subscribe to many of the myths and fallacies outlined in this book.

People have to be taught to fall in love; it is not an instinct or automatic process. Our romantic education comes from several sources — parents, playmates, books, magazines, movies, television, popular songs. Media images emphasize rapture as the index of a successful marriage. The love bond becomes idealized and the partners "worship" each other.

This mythical romantic tradition has a number of allies. *Love at first sight* is one of the prominent romantic themes. Anyone who understands the meaning of love will realize that this complex emotion requires the passage of time for its development. Infatuation, or physical attraction is certainly possible at first sight. But love comes from the discovery of qualities that are lovable, and from a shared togetherness that lends fulfillment and mutual enrichment.

Falling madly in love is another phrase that is heard all too often. Popular songs, "confession" magazines, and many movies aid and abet the delusion that the dream of true romantic love can be attained and sustained. One problem is that people whose major aim is to love and be loved tend to neglect the development of other aspects of their lives. They may neglect the very skills and resources that would enhance their genuine interpersonal attractiveness or "loveability." People tend to grow weary of each other's company unless they have cultivated common interests and values. Romantic love is passionate and fiery. It soon burns out. Conjugal affection is a slow-burning, heart warming flame that brings security and comfort.

In the early months and years of marriage, partners inevitably discover that their spouses do not have the attributes of their dream heroes and heroines. Most are able to adjust to this reality, but extreme romantics are unable to do so. The male romantic idealist searches fruitlessly for a mate who will provide the tenderness, the security and the solicitude of the ideal mother, as well as the ecstatic sexual joys of a fantasy sweetheart. The romantic woman wants her man to be the ideal father, husband, caretaker, companion, and lover, all rolled into one. Viewed from a clinical perspective, these perceptions are decidedly abnormal. Indeed, the very language of romantic love attests to the psychotic quality of the interaction. She is "crazy" about him; he is "mad" about her. In the throes of this all-consuming passion, otherwise rational and responsible people have been known to cast aside, quite recklessly, all obligations to family, friends and society.

Millions of adolescents and adults still read romantic pulp stories that fill their heads with yarns about princes eloping with go-go dancers or secretaries, or the beautiful heiress who marries her handsome chauffeur. In keeping with democratic ideals, each of us can choose anyone to meet, fall in love with, marry. Little attention is paid to the fact that people whose backgrounds are extremely different seldom see eye-to-eye on important matters. I have been struck by the fact that when a man whose family has money marries a woman from modest financial circumstances (or vice versa), the difference in their views of money often becomes a stumbling block. Similarly, when a well-educated woman, whose parents and siblings are all professionals, marries a man who dropped out of high school, we can predict with uncanny accuracy that academic credentials (or the lack thereof) will probably become a bone of contention. The Cinderella theme is a good fairy story, but in real life, Prince Charming is more likely than not to discover that their unequal stations will cause grief and estrangement. (See Myth 21).

There are many societies that do not base marriages on romance but on prearranged unions. Such marriages are organized by parents or other responsible family members who select the mate, not on capricious whims, but on the basis of similar cultural, social and class interests. Arranged marriages are still very much in vogue throughout India and the Orient.

While we balk at the idea of abandoning our romantic idealism, much emotional pain would be spared if more people knew how to replace romantic love with conjugal affection as the basis for a truly successful marriage. The affection that enables a marriage to endure is something finer, deeper, and more rewarding than the romantic love of the storybooks.

Conjugal caring and affection cannot exist without mutual evidence of several key qualities:

- kindness
- consideration/communication
- harmonious adjustment to each other's habits
- joint participation in several activities
- consensus on important values and issues
- reciprocity rather than coercion, and
- clear evidence of respect for one another.

Married couples must adjust to daily routines of dressing, eating, working, sleeping and similar habits that call for synchronous schedules, and countless activities that become conditioned to each other. The aim is to build up a "common capital" of acts, habits and experiences that result in a profound acceptance of each other, without the false hopes and impossible illusions of the romantic ideal.

MYTH 2 REVISITED

Here I agree entirely with what I had written and can neither add nor subtract anything.

MYTH 3

Extramarital Affairs Will Destroy a Marriage

onventional wisdom decrees that a happily married man would not fall in love with, or leave his wife for, another woman. Similarly, no wife would jeopardize a happy marriage by becoming sexually involved with another man. Thus, having an affair is proof in itself that something must be lacking in the marriage.

Not true!

People get involved in extramarital relations for a variety of reasons, only some of which are a reflection of marital defects or distress. Sexually frustrated husbands or wives tend to seek from others what they cannot obtain from their spouses. In other cases, the problem resides not in the marriage, but in the individual partner. Some people, for instance, are unsure of their own physical attractiveness and sexual prowess, and elect to keep proving their desirability and skill in bed. Other people are perhaps so very highly sexed that few can keep pace with them.

A man once said to me: "Show me a person who is having an affair and I will show you a marriage that is on the rocks!" It turned out that he had been married three times and that each of his wives had left him for their respective lovers. But I know several men and women whose extramarital involvements were purely an

17

expression of curiosity, personal growth, an antidote for boredom, or the manifestation of a varietal disposition. The point is that there are both healthy and unhealthy reasons for having extramarital relations.

A man or a woman who, in thirty years of marriage, was never tempted to have an extramarital interlude and had no desire to find out how it would feel to have sex with someone other than his or her spouse, may be suspected of being biologically and psychologically abnormal. A married person who occasionally and unobtrusively had experienced sexual intercourse outside the marriage, would be well within the normally expressive range. Many men and women are ripe for a new adventure, whether they realize it or not. A friend of mine, on the occasion of his twenty-fifth wedding anniversary, told me that he had been having discreet affairs for the past 24 years, and added that his sex life at home was still the best. He intended to keep the marital bed exciting, he said, by continuing to have discreet affairs until his golden wedding anniversary!

This is not meant to imply that extramarital sex will necessarily enhance most people's marriages. There are those for whom sex outside the confines of marriage would be clearly inadvisable, if not unthinkable, because of temperament, religious upbringing, or social conditioning. I have seen people consumed by guilt after indulging in illicit sex. My advice has been to avoid future liaisons as if they were chocolate brownies laced with arsenic. For some, extramarital sex can be pure poison!

The other side of the coin is exemplified by a true story that goes back to 1960. I had recently launched into full-time private practice, and one of my first patients was a 30-year-old woman, married for five years and mother of a four-year-old and a two-year-old. Anita was thinking of leaving her husband, but before seeing a lawyer, she decided to consult a psychologist to determine whether the marriage could be saved. The major problem, she said, had existed from the wedding day. For her husband, sex once a month — or even once every couple of months — was more than sufficient. She described herself as "hot-blooded," and capable of passionate intercourse every night, if not twice a night.

Full evaluation and possible treatment for the problem would have required meeting with her husband. When I explained the need for couple's therapy, the husband refused to see me. He took the position that there was nothing wrong with him: Anita was over-sexed. Upon hearing this, she decided to sue for divorce.

I cautioned her not to be hasty, and asked several questions. Apart from sexual incompatibility, what was he like as a husband in general? She described him as kind, hard-working, concerned, caring, good-natured, and dependable. What sort of father was he? He was a fine father who helped with the children, spent time with them, loved them and was loved by them. And what sort of a provider was he? Excellent! He was Vice-President of a large and growing company, had a lucrative profit-sharing plan, drew a high salary, and had several substantial investments. What sort of a companion was he? Although he worked hard, he was no work-aholic, and he found time for social gatherings, interesting vacations and other recreational pursuits.

When I asked why she was willing to give up so much, and to break up a family, all for the sake of sex, Anita grew angry and snapped at me: "It's all very easy for you to talk! Are you climbing the walls out of frustration?"

Since her husband appeared to have so many positive attributes, such rare qualities, I suggested she consider continuing the marriage while finding sexual gratification elsewhere. "But that's downright immoral!" she countered. Was it, I inquired, more moral to get divorced, break up a family, separate father and children and destroy what sounded like a good relationship? (She had mentioned that the only tensions that entered into the marriage centered around their sexual differences.)

"Thou shalt not commit adultery!" was her fiery retort. But was the intent of the commandment not to preserve and protect marriages and families? Since an outside association might prevent a divorce and preserve the family, the emphasis here was not on ordinary adultery, but on benevolent adultery.

Several weeks later, Anita seduced Neil, her partner in a mixed doubles tennis tournament, and entered into a "hot and heavy affair." Her lover, ten years her senior, had three children and a wife who had been paraplegic since sustaining spinal injuries in a car accident two years previously.

Three years into the affair Anita was back in my office. Some difficulties had arisen when Neil started pressuring her to marry him. I met with the couple and pointed out to Neil that if he abandoned his helpless wife, he would be so consumed by guilt that this would destroy a second marriage. "And if you were *not* consumed with guilt, I would want nothing more to do with such a cold-hearted bastard!" Anita exclaimed.

In 1980, while carrying out follow-up investigations, I found that their extramarital relationship was still going strong. Two marriages and two families had been saved. Neil's children were all married and he was a grandfather. Anita's son was in graduate school and her daughter, who was engaged to be married, was working in her father's company.

Extramarital sex enhances some marriages, makes absolutely no difference to others, and can also prove to be downright destructive. But it is a myth that these outside liaisons *inevitably* undermine the quality and security of marriage; nor are they proof positive that "something is wrong" with the marriage.

MYTH 3 REVISITED

I regret having included this myth in the book because it has been misunderstood by many. "Lazarus recommends extramarital sex to the nation" some incorrectly concluded. The point I wanted to emphasize is that, on occasion, an extramarital liaison has been known to have helped or even saved some marriages. I was interested in challenging the idea that an affair will *always* destroy a marriage, and that it *always* meant that the marriage per se was defective and impaired. Clearly, the virtues of faithfulness, loyalty, devotion, fidelity and trustworthiness can hardly be over-emphasized. "Anita's" story is interesting and provocative, but on the whole, this myth is one of the less significant ones in the book and could easily have been dropped. As a colleague pointed out, had it not appeared originally, *Marital Myths* would have been more acceptable to schools and religious groups!

Extramarital sex can be helpful to some (very few) marriages, but in general, the monogamous thrust of our society is such that it is more likely to be detrimental.

MYTH 4

If You Feel Guilty, Confess

This myth is potentially more dangerous than several of the others put together. In Myth 1, I referred to the strain that "total openness" can impose on a marriage: whereas special friendships can proceed all the way from A to Z, good marriages should probably stop at W. Z-type information can overload a marriage. Revelations about extramarital involvements, for example — be they one night stands or enduring passionate affairs — fall into the Z category.

Some years ago, when discussing this issue in a "Marriage and Sex Therapy" class, one of the students claimed that my bias reflected my age and the different generation I represent. He insisted that the young marrieds of today, unlike their parents, are often quite willing to accept "open marriage." He claimed that jealousy is a relic of an era in which marriage had been equated with ownership. He boasted that both he and his wife knew of one another's affairs, past and present, and that this knowledge, far from damaging their marriage, served to enhance it: "In fact, we like to tell one another what we do in bed with other people. This is a strong turn-on for us both, and makes our own sex more exciting and enjoyable." This led to a heated discussion, with most of his peers disagreeing with his point of view. Two years later, I heard that he was divorced and had remarried.

There are no hard and fast rules that pertain to all marriages. People are complex and diverse. I am sure that there must be those for whom open marriage, swinging groups, or communal living will enrich rather than destroy their relationships. But my observations of clients and acquaintances, close and distant, have led me to conclude that if most marriages are to remain viable, certain matters are best kept to oneself.

A good example concerns a young college professor who had become involved with a female student. Jeff was happily married to Linda, but unable to resist the charms of a particularly attractive sophomore who flattered him, boosted his ego, and finally taught him a thing or two in bed. Their clandestine romance continued over two semesters and Jeff became more deeply attached to his paramour than he had anticipated. Since he truly loved Linda and their two young babies, he decided to terminate the affair. A couple of months later, still feeling sad that a "beautiful relationship" had ended, and also feeling upset and somewhat confused, he consulted a counselor. He was advised to "come clean" and tell Linda what he had been doing. (This counselor subscribed to two other marital myths: *Husband and wife should keep no secrets from each other;* and *In marriage, total honesty is the best policy.*)

Jeff followed his counselor's advice and told his wife about his *affair d'amour.* He "owned up," and Linda reacted with what only can be described as "psychotic fury." The poor fellow found himself the recipient of such a vicious vendetta that his needs might have been better served had he cut out his tongue. By the time Linda and her influential father were done with him, Jeff had no wife, no girlfriend, no job, and no access to his children.

Many men have told me of a fantasy of a devoted and totally faithful wife who not only condones extramarital escapades, but actually applauds them. If things go wrong with their mistresses, they want to be able to turn to their wives for solace. I have treated many a man who was crazy enough to try to put this fantasy into operation, and felt extremely put out when his wife was unsympathetic.

Here is a typical example: Kate and Joanne had been best friends since high school. They both got married in college and their friendship continued unchanged. Four years later, Kate got divorced and Joanne and her husband Stan both gave her the emotional support she required. Soon, Kate and Stan got closer, and they added sex to their good friendship. A few weeks later, Stan told Joanne about his sexual involvement with her best friend, fully expecting her understanding and approval. Instead, Joanne reacted tearfully and angrily, insisting that she had been betrayed. Stan was nonplussed. As he expressed it to me, "It's not as though I had gone out and picked up a stranger!"

Stan's naivete is by no means as rare as one might suppose. I have heard similar stories dozens of times.

A widely prevalent myth, especially among mental health practitioners (who should know better!) is that *There is nothing in a marriage which the other spouse doesn't know on some level.* Thus, according to this notion, no important secrets are possible. If a husband is seeing another woman, the wife knows about it somewhere in her "unconscious mind." If a wife has a lover, the husband is bound to register subliminal signals and end up knowing, on some level, about his wife's encounters. I strongly dispute these opinions. Let me cite an example.

Several years ago, a friend of mine was having an affair. Harry was rather indiscreet, if not flagrant, and many people knew about it. Ellen was one of his employees. Consequently, she was often a guest in his home on the pretext of having come over to assist him with work. His wife, Barbara, and Ellen sometimes went shopping together, and on occasion, the three of them went to the movies together. This continued for over four years and was often the talk of the town. A question that everyone pondered was whether or not Barbara knew what was going on. "Surely she knows what's happening." "Who can be so blind?" "They probably have a *ménage à trois.*" I was the only one who insisted that from all I had observed, Barbara had no idea of the true nature of their relationship.

To assuage his guilt feelings, Harry decided to tell Barbara the truth. I think he wanted to end the affair and realized that this would undoubtedly achieve that end. His confession had a devastating impact from which the couple (and Ellen) are still reeling. I waited a few weeks for some of the sparks to stop flying, and asked Barbara if she had suspected the truth at some level of her thinking or feeling. It would have been a face-saving ploy to have told me that she is not naive, that of course she had had her suspicions. "I had absolutely no idea whatsoever," she told me. "First of all I trusted Harry implicitly." (See Myth 7.) "And besides, I felt sorry for Ellen. She's had a hard life, and I automatically thought that Harry felt similarly." Harry recently told me that he'd give "just about anything" to be able to erase knowledge of the affair from Barbara's mind.

If you feel guilty over an affair, it is best to come clean and confess the whole thing to someone *other* than your spouse (someone you can trust to keep a confidence).

MYTH 4 REVISITED

I can't say it too often — those who believe that a couple should be completely transparent and totally open with one another will often court disaster. Recently, a physician who had ended an affair with one of his nurses decided that it would be most honorable to inform his wife of his infidelity (she had no idea that he had been unfaithful). I asked him what he thought this would accomplish. "First off," said he, "I will feel better getting it off my chest and out of my conscience, and secondly, it will prove to my wife that she can really trust me from now on." I said I failed to comprehend any logic behind his reasoning and I cautioned him that dire repercussions would probably result from such disclosures. I virtually implored him to live with his guilt, learn from his dalliance, and invest more time and energy into ensuring that his marriage would go forward. He did not heed my advice. His wife was devastated by his revelation, and after more than a year of couples therapy they parted company. "I should have followed your advice," he told me. "I'll never find someone even half as wonderful as my ex-wife!"

Being too open with your spouse is more than likely to damage your relationship.

Husbands and Wives Should Do Everything Together

The "total togetherness" myth is one of the most prevalent. It probably springs from the romantic fallacy (Myth 2) in which the ideal matrimonial union consists of two separate individuals merging into one ecstatic entity. The two "love birds" go everywhere together, do everything together, share everything together. To have any noteworthy experiences without the other is unthinkable. They stop functioning as individuals, and interact only as a couple. When discussing these matters with my clients, the following simple diagrams have proved useful:

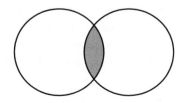

This depicts a poor marriage relationship. There is very little togetherness or common ground.

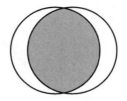

*This depicts an excellent marriage. There is about 75–80
percent togetherness but also sufficient separateness to
permit individual growth and essential privacy.*

*This represents the romantic ideal where two people merge
so completely that they become as one. In practice, were this possible,
it would probably result in emotional suffocation.*

In my opinion, most married people have transferred responsibility from their parents to their spouses. When six-year-old Pat asks seven-year-old Kim if he can come over and play, little Kim appropriately answers "I'll have to ask my mommy." When twenty-six-year-old Pat asks twenty-seven-year-old Kim if he would like to go bowling, to a football game, or to a horror movie that their wives would detest, it strikes me as absurd for him to say, "I'll have to ask my wife." It is even more absurd when twenty-five-year-old Alice is invited to go to the opera (which she loves and her husband hates) and says, "I'll have to see if my husband will let me go."

I am not advocating an irresponsible, couldn't-care-less attitude. Clearly, an effective partnership implies that the other person will be given due consideration. Thus, when Sam announces to Suzie that he is going bowling with the boys, and she says, "Did you forget that we promised to visit Aunt Tilly in the hospital?" Sam explains to this friends that he won't be joining them that night, not because his keeper won't let him out, but because he had made a prior commitment. Similarly, if Suzie feels like spending time with her friends, or seeing the ballet, she states her intentions, and certainly does not ask if Sam will grant permission, or "let her go."

Am I just splitting hairs? I think not. People have countered by explaining: "When I say, "I'll have to ask my wife,' I don't mean that I need my "mother's' blessings. I just don't think it's good to make unilateral decisions in marriage, so we first check things out with each other."

("Don't make unilateral decisions" could be another myth on the list. Of course major decisions that have an impact on the marriage in general or on the spouse in particular are best made jointly. To avoid all unilateral decisions, however, is to stop thinking independently.)

Speech often reveals basic thought and action. "Asking" is very different from "telling." Getting permission is not the same as determining whether good reasons exist for changing a course of action. "My husband doesn't allow me to go out at night." "My wife won't let me join a health club." "She won't hear of me playing golf on weekends." "He doesn't let me play tournament bridge." These are literal quotes, culled from my case notes on people who were in marriage therapy precisely because one or both parties exerted undue pressures to remain a twosome, and granted one another very little freedom of movement. No wonder many people perceive marriage as bondage and remain terrified at the prospect!

Humorous quips about marriage and divorce are abundant: "When a marriage ends in divorce, it's merely another fight that didn't go the distance." "Marriage is usually due to lack of judgement, divorce to lack of patience, and remarriage to lack of memory." "Insanity is grounds for divorce in some states, but grounds for marriage in all."

Cartoonists very often depict marriage in terms of a ball-and-chain. Too bad! A good marriage actually increases one's freedom. Here is a true-to-life example: Millie, after playing Bunco with "the girls," returned home to find that her husband (who had stayed home to do some paperwork) had unpacked the dishwasher, and had done two loads of laundry. The next night, he returned home from a poker game with "the boys" to find that Millie had painted the guest room (a job that he was dreading and had put off until the weekend).

Some people feel guilty when they do things, or go places without their husbands or wives. "I don't think it's right or proper for a husband to go one way and a wife another. If they want to act like single people, why did they get married?" This statement came from forty-four-year-old Alf who insisted that his wife should go boating with him. Marie preferred reading a book on the beach while he was out on the boat. She said "I get seasick. I'm not stopping him from going on the boat. Is it asking too much for Alf to do what he enjoys, while I do what I enjoy? After he docks the boat, we can always have a drink on board and then go out for dinner." Alf found this unacceptable. "All the other men go out with their wives. I like doing things as a twosome."

Steve had similar ideas, but in his case, he believed in having family togetherness. Also a boating man, his picture of family solidarity was that of Janet and their two sons on board while he steered his $96,000 vessel around the bay. His wife and their younger son enjoyed swimming, surfing, or merely taking long walks on the beach. So why not go boating with the older boy, while Janet and Billy did their own thing? "That's not my idea of fun or a family outing," Steve explained.

Alf and Steve both used coercion in their marriages. It is not a good idea to bring pressure to bear on one's marriage partner. Most people strongly dislike being pushed and pressured into something they'd rather not do. The inevitable resentments that arise tend to create marital strife and tensions. Alf and Steve did not even offer acceptable trade-offs. They could have said something such as: "It's important enough to me that you do this, that I promise to get tickets for three Broadway plays over the next two months, *and* I will take you out to four fancy restaurants between Labor Day and Christmas."

Cocktail parties had become a bone of contention with a couple I was seeing for marriage therapy. Fred hated them; Kay loved them. Fred declared: "I'd rather stay home, watch television, or read a book. I hate making small talk." Kay said: "I find them a wonderful opportunity to dress up, meet new people, run into old friends, and keep up with the local gossip." She usually managed to cajole her husband into going with her, but at times they almost came to blows. He often tried to sabotage matters by picking a fight just before it was time to get dressed. This is what I advised:

AAL: (To Fred): Tell me honestly, would you object if she went to these parties alone, so you could stay home and relax instead of being dragged there kicking and screaming?

Fred: Would I object? Hell no! I'd love it.

AAL: (Addressing Kay): It seems that you pay a steep price for having him as your escort. Why not go without him?

Kay: How could I do that? What would people think? What would I say if they asked where he is?

AAL: You could say he's out of town, or he's not feeling well, or he had important business to attend to. You could also simply tell them the truth, that he dislikes cocktail parties and that you two have agreed that he doesn't have to accompany you.

Kay took my advice, not only in reference to cocktail parties, but also with regard to shows that she wished to see and which Fred had no interest in seeing (in which case she either went along with another couple, or with one or more friends). The result was a new found freedom for both, fewer conflicts and a closer marriage.

I'd like to mention one other case before turning to the next myth. A couple consulted me because their marriage was on the rocks; the husband had already spoken to a lawyer. The wife was extremely distressed and described herself as depressed and anxious over the impending breakup of the marriage. They had four children ranging in age from ten years to four-and-a-half. Husband Jason explained his position as follows: "I don't know what it is. I'm very confused. I love Laura and the kids, but everything is just too much for me. I feel I've got to get away before I go crazy or have a heart attack."

The main problem became obvious to me after seeing Jason and Laura individually. The marriage had much to commend it, but Laura was overwhelming Jason with togetherness. She was a great planner who loved to orchestrate her family into a team that, as her husband saw it, placed too many demands on his time. Step one in saving this worthwhile marriage was to exclude daddy from various parent-child activities. Step two came from Jason: "I feel the need to spend one night a week away from home. I'd just like to check into a motel, *alone,* take some paperwork from the office, a good book, have some dinner, go to the room *alone,* relax, take a hot bath, watch some TV. My wife and kids can have me six nights, but I want that seventh to myself."

Laura was not exactly thrilled at the prospect and suspected that he was really devising a scheme to spend that night out with another woman. As far as I could determine, he was truly interested in solitude, rest, peace, and some private emotional and physical space. I stressed that by insisting on seven out of seven, she *may* end up with zero, but by agreeing to six out of seven, the marriage might be saved, and its quality could very well be enhanced.

That was over ten years ago. It worked, and has kept on working. The slight adjustment in the amount of togetherness versus aloneness prevented a basically good marriage from turning bad. Laura still suspects that on his night out, Jason probably spends time with another woman: "I'm not absolutely sure of this, and what I don't know can't hurt me, but I must admit that he's been infinitely easier to live with, and that we have a very good marriage."

MYTH 5 REVISITED

I regard this as one of the most important myths in the book. Again and again I have seen couples whose relationship deteriorated because they had over dosed on each other. It is wise to guard against too much of a good thing! There are exceptions to most rules. Thus, we probably all know some couples who seem to be joined at the hip, who are held up as examples of love birds who go everywhere together, do everything together, and are never apart, and appear to thrive on it. Apart from the fact that I contend that such intense mutual dependency is unhealthy for many reasons, the couples who thrive on so much propinquity are in the vast minority.

- Never relinquish your individuality, but learn to be a team player and cooperate with your partner. If you maintain a 20-25% level of separation, this will keep the 75% level of togetherness alive and well.

MYTH 6

You Have To Work at Marriage

We are told that good things do not come easily. We are supposed to expend effort to gain something worthwhile. Things that are achieved too easily will not be valued, wanted or respected. These cliches have a profound effect on the attitudes and values of many people in our society. While they probably hold up on the athletic field, their extension into the domain of human relationships has had some unfortunate consequences.

Marriage has often (incorrectly) been equated to a garden. A beautiful garden calls for effort: planning, development, cultivation, and maintenance. One is unlikely to win the "Beautiful Gardens" competition simply by tossing around some grass seed and turning on a sprinkler from time to time. It calls for sustained effort to till the ground, feed and fertilize the soil, prune, and trim.

Should marriage be any different? Can a good marriage be attained and maintained without ongoing effort? Surely not! Do you not have to strive and keep on striving for anything worthwhile? Isn't marriage hard work?

If work means constantly putting the other person's needs before your own; being a good listener into the early hours of the morning; being understanding, supportive, and loveable at all times; trying not to say or do anything that your partner will find offensive — I say "Forget it!" Unfortunately, many people expect nothing less than hard labor.

Marriage calls for adjustment — and readjustment — which is different from work. Two people from different families, with unique combinations of genes and chromosomes, varied social and psychological experiences, join in holy matrimony and adjust to one another's idiosyncracies. This leads to a basic truth. *All good marriages are based on compromise.*

In a happy, successful marriage, people *share* each other's lives; they don't *run* each other's lives (see Myth 20). It helps to be a good negotiator. Thus, it is no myth to assert that a good marriage requires some effort. When does effort become hard work? Perhaps the following case history will bring home the difference.

Maurice and Carol's whirlwind romance resulted in marriage within three-and-a-half weeks. Their problems surfaced on the honeymoon. He discovered a fondness for sailing and she found that boats made her seasick. She wished to socialize with other couples; he wanted her company alone. He wanted to make love in the early morning; she was a "night person." Six months later their catalog of personal differences had escalated from minor skirmishes to major conflicts. They often felt hurt, angry, and misunderstood by each other. Like many couples, they fought, but they also had good times of joy, laughter, and happiness. After 14 months their daughter was born. By their third anniversary, Maurice and Carol's marriage had grown so stormy that the topic of "divorce" became a reality rather than a casual threat. They were disagreeing and exploding at one another even in public. But before consulting lawyers en route to the divorce court, "marriage counseling" seemed a more logical and constructive step. They telephoned for an appointment.

I saw the couple a few times and then met with Maurice and Carol separately for two sessions. I pinpointed their main areas of disagreement, their faulty tactics for dealing with conflict, and their ineffective methods of attempting to resolve their differences. We dwelled on constructive methods of reaching specific agreements, developing contractual arrangements, avoiding hidden agendas, and forming open negotiations.

Carol pinned the following list on the bulletin board in the kitchen:

1. Never criticize a person; only criticize a specific aspect of his/her behavior.
2. Don't "mind-rape" (that is, do not tell the other person what he/she is thinking or feeling).
3. Avoid saying "You always..." "You never..." Be specific.
4. Avoid right-wrong, good-bad categories. When differences arise, look for compromises.
5. Use "I feel" messages instead of "You are" messages. For example, say: "I feel hurt when you ignore me!" Do not say "You are selfish and inconsiderate for ignoring me."
6. Be direct and honest. Say what you mean, and mean what you say.
7. I'm okay, you're okay. I count, you count.

Carol made two additional copies of these "Seven Basic Ground Rules." Maurice kept one in his wallet and Carol put the other in her pocketbook.

Our weekly therapy sessions enabled the couple to implement these guidelines and to develop additional do's and don'ts for a successful marriage. After four months of therapy Maurice and Carol had stopped fighting. No harsh words passed between them. Carol reported: "We've hardly fought over the past five or six weeks, and we have managed to compromise and negotiate right down the line." Maurice agreed. He added, "We debate rather than argue, and we draw up contracts with each other whenever differences arise." Carol remarked that they had never related so well — not even during their brief but romantic courtship.

At this juncture it appeared that counseling had been a success. In place of coercion we had achieved reciprocity. Quarrels and combative dealings had been replaced by discussion and fair play. Carol commented, "But it's such hard work!" Maurice looked at me and said, "Well, I guess a good marriage is something you have to work at. They say it's like a garden that must be watered and weeded and fertilized. Good marriages don't just happen. They are created. Right?"

Before I could say anything, Carol spoke up: "When we first came to you about four months ago we were in a canoe about to plunge over the rapids. You gave us paddles. Now we have rowed pretty far upstream. But the current is so strong that we dare not relax and enjoy the scenery. If we stop paddling, even for a few minutes, we will be swept downstream and go right over the rapids!"

I looked at Maurice. Our eyes met and then he looked away. Carol stared at the ceiling. She seemed deep in thought. Their words were touching off something in my own feelings; I felt uneasy. "Good marriages require hard work!" "We dare not relax!" "The current is so strong!" "It's like a garden that must be fertilized!" I had spent more than a dozen hours with this young couple, and now we had reached a turning point. They were excellent clients who had carried out their assignments and had made enormous progress. Now they were questioning the results. They were afraid to ask the basic questions that were implied by their remarks. "Is this all there is to marriage?" "Have we gone and traded our noisy battles for hard labor?"

I decided to be completely outspoken. "Well, perhaps the two of you are now ripe and ready for an amicable divorce."

Neither Carol nor Maurice seemed taken aback by this comment. If anything, they both appeared somewhat relieved that I was willing to stop touting the virtues of togetherness and endless compromise. As Carol put it, "We have to haggle over almost every decision." Maurice loved watching television; Carol hated it. She loved ballet and opera; he found them boring. He liked softball, bowling, handball; she liked tennis, golf and swimming. Thus, practically every separate or mutual activity called for some form of negotiation and compromise. "I'll go to the ballet if you are willing to go to a movie." "Why don't you play tennis while I go bowling?" As we discussed additional likes and dislikes it became apparent that Maurice and Carol disagreed about almost everything. They had different tastes in clothes, people, art, food, politics and religion. Yet sexually they had developed a sustained and satisfying relationship. "The only place we really agree is in bed."

Despite these vast differences, marriage therapy had enabled Carol and Maurice to live together without colliding. They handled their disagreements maturely, rationally, and quite sensibly. But now I saw why they both found their marriage so enervating and tedious. They did not have a marriage. They had a well-functioning uphill partnership. They had sex, but they were not lovers. They did not have companionship or mutual happiness. In one another's company they experienced a few harmonious situations but remained feeling desperately alone. This marriage, in fact, should never have taken place.

Maurice asked: "But shouldn't we stay together for the sake of our child? You know what happens to kids from broken homes!" I pointed out that I have treated dozens of adults whose problems stemmed from the fact that their parents had remained married "for the sake of the children." Many adult patients have said: "I wish my parents had gotten divorced, I'd have been much better off." It is not a good idea to raise a child in an atmosphere of tension and guarded affection, or worse, in a household where parents create strife and conflict. An amicable divorce, wherein the children have easy access to both parents, provides a much healthier climate for psychological growth. (See Myth 15)

The decision to get divorced seldom comes easily. Carol and Maurice spent the next couple of months thinking it over. They called for an appointment. "It's no use," Carol reported, "although we're still getting along just fine, we really don't have enough in common to make it work." I said that a good time to implement an amicable divorce is when the marriage is relatively smooth rather than stormy. "It's so much easier to be fair, rational and open-minded about divorce settlements when you are friends rather than foes." Maurice said, "Actually we make a good couple of friends but a rotten pair of spouses."

The three of us worked out an equitable divorce agreement. Maurice and Carol would have joint custody of their daughter. We discussed the division of finances, furniture and other possessions, and new accommodations. Lawyers drew up the final agreement and, 18 months later, Maurice and Carol's "no fault" divorce was granted.

Almost five years have passed since I last saw them. I tracked down Maurice at his place of work for a follow-up. He married about seven months after the divorce, and Carol remarried a few months after him. They each had another child. Maurice said that his second marriage was most rewarding. "I learned from my mistakes the first time around, and as far as I know, Carol is also doing just fine." Their daughter, now seven years old, enjoyed "mothering" her respective half-brother and half-sister. "I'm pleased to report that she is really a happy child... I know we did the right thing."

What Can We Learn from Carol and Maurice?
Some authorities believe that almost any two people can make a go of marriage if they follow basic ground rules.

Avoid: labeling; blaming, judging; accusing; fault-finding; demanding; ignoring; attacking.

Include: praising; complimenting; listening; discussing; thanking; helping; forgiving.

By adhering to these guidelines, a successful, happy marriage is almost guaranteed. *Nonsense!* While radical behavioral scientists object to intangibles such as "love" and "physical chemistry," most of us realize that there is a vast difference between a peaceful and friendly coexistence and a successful or worthwhile marriage. Marriage therapy converted Carol and Maurice's abrasive and offensive relationship into a tiring armistice, replete with negotiations over trivial decisions. Yet they remained fundamentally incompatible. Like-minded interests and mutual agreements were almost nonexistent.

Marriage requires a partnership, teamwork, common goals, and respectful dealings, but it is far more than the sum of these parts. Without love, affection, attraction, caring and understanding, plus some consensus in matters of taste and interest, marriage is as arid as the sands of the Sahara.

I asked Maurice to elaborate on his second marriage. His major lesson from the marital therapy was to find a woman who shared his interests, who respected his tastes, and vice versa. When asked if he was "working at" his second marriage, whether it required constant attention like a garden, he said: "Hell no! We just get along." He added that while he and his wife have certain differences, over which they negotiate and compromise quite rationally, the basic tenor of their relationship was one of "mutualism." He then reflected: "Perhaps the idea that you have to work at creating a good marriage stems from the fact that most married couples are incompatible."

MYTH 6 REVISITED

As Dr. Sam Hamburg emphasizes in his excellent book *Will Our Love Last?* truly happy marriages involve couples who (1) see eye-to-eye on the practical details of life, (2) are on the same wavelength, and (3) have similar sexual needs and preferences. When it requires hard work to keep a marriage afloat, this points to the fact that incompatibilities exist in one or more of the above-mentioned dimensions.

One of the most significant problems on the practical dimension involves money. Different views on the importance of money, on spending habits, and on saving money always spell trouble. Likewise, neatness (or the lack thereof) also often plays a major role. The wavelength dimension involves values, aspirations, ambitions, spiritual orientations, and political leanings. These are a few of the main factors, and any discords will undermine the quality of the relationship. In every marriage, differences are bound to arise and thus it will be necessary to expend effort to deal with various issues. If this effort amounts to hard labor, it signifies a basic incompatibility, and the couple will need to determine if the pros nevertheless outweigh the cons.

I agree with Dr. Hamburg that the key to a happy marriage is to choose someone with whom you are deeply compatible in the first place.

MYTH 7

A Happy Marriage Requires Total Trust

*A*nything taken to excess tends to be unfortunate. If one is too tall, too thin, too clever, too fussy, the implication is that one would be better off with less of that particular attribute. Being *too trusting*, for example, can prove disastrous.

When I was in college, one of my friends was a second-year medical student named Gary, who had been married for about six months. I noticed that Gary's wife spent a lot of time in the company of a particular young man, and I commented to my friend that he was asking for trouble. "Oh come now," he protested, "Mike and I have been pals for years. I have a lot of studying to do, so why should I expect Sue to sit at home and twiddle her thumbs? I asked Mike if he would mind entertaining Sue a few nights a week. This way she gets to see movies, goes to parties, and I don't have to feel guilty while studying." I pointed out that Mike was good looking, well-off financially (he had joined his wealthy father in business), and far too available. Gary insisted that he trusted both Mike and Sue implicitly. Alas, after a very short while, Sue informed Gary that she and Mike had fallen in love, and asked for a divorce.

Another, and more personal, vignette goes back to the early years of my own marriage. My wife and I had moved into a new house. I returned home from work to find a gentleman enjoying a drink with my wife in the living room. "This is Charles," she said, "he lives four houses down and came over to welcome us to the neighborhood." How very kind and thoughtful. I chatted with Charles, offered him another beer, and when he left, thanked him for his good neighborliness. When I returned home the next day to find Charles in my home again, I decided there and then that he was abusing the Welcome Wagon. I told him so in no uncertain terms. Whether or not anything might have developed between Charles and my wife is beside the point. Those of us who don't believe in blind or total trust prefer to nip potential trouble in the bud.

Shirley had been married to Don for nearly twelve years. She had no reason not to trust him or to suspect that he was involved with another woman. Suddenly, this very astute wife noticed two tell-tale signs. Don, who had hardly ever watched anything but market reports and football on TV began to develop a taste for evening soap operas. A conservative dresser, he came home with three outlandish ties. "To me, this added up to the beginnings of an actual or potential affair. The time to act was *now*, so that I could stop it before it got started, or before it developed into a heavy romance." Shirley's investigations and observations pointed to a petite young receptionist who had recently joined Don's company. Shirley considered confronting the young receptionist, but decided that it would be better to discuss the matter with Don. It appeared that the relationship was still in the stages of an early flirtation. The receptionist finally lost her job, but Shirley's absence of total trust possibly saved the marriage. She and Don then worked with me to upgrade the quality of their relationship.

My fourth anecdote concerns a conversation that took place in the men's locker room at a country club. As I stepped out of the sauna into the showers, three men were discussing whether or not their wives might be "unfaithful." One of the men was saying that although, in his fifteen years of marriage, he had no cause to doubt his wife's faithfulness, one could never be one hundred per cent sure of anything. Another fellow agreed and added that he was about ninety per cent certain that his wife had not, and would not, have sex with another man, except under the most unusual circumstances — such as being snowbound for three weeks with Robert Redford. The third man said that he was absolutely, one hundred per cent positive that his wife would not have extramarital sex under any circumstances. He referred to her strict religious upbringing, to the fact that she was a prude, basically uninterested in sex, extremely shy and inhibited, and besides, she was far too concerned about public opinion to take such a risk. He added that there was not one chance in ten million that his wife would be capable of "cheating." At this point in the conversation I realized that the last speaker was the husband of one of my patients. His wife was in fact involved in a sexual affair, which was why she came to me for psychotherapy.

Good marriages tend to be based not on total trust, but on a tinge of insecurity. To be absolutely certain of a spouse's fidelity, loyalty, or devotion, is to take the other person too much for granted. Too much certainty breeds a subtle lack of respect. It is more realistic to believe that one's partner is a faithful fallible human being who can succumb to temptation under certain circumstances. Unless one exercises a certain degree of vigilance, it is possible to be usurped or replaced.

The "market value" that one places on one's husband or wife is another important factor. If you regard your spouse as too homely to attract another worthwhile person, your total trust and complete security will not generate very much respect, excitement, or satisfaction. On the other hand, if you consider your spouse quite capable of attracting members of the opposite sex, and liable to respond to these overtures if neglected or mistreated inside the marriage, you will likely increase your own attentiveness and displays of caring and affection.

The "tinge of insecurity" keeps a marriage viable, meaningful, even exciting. It prevents one from taking things for granted, growing fat or sloppy, paying more attention to the job than necessary, or displaying disrespect. What is more, it fosters and maintains the level of love and affectionate caring that makes marriage worth preserving.

MYTH 7 REVISITED

The total trust misconception has continued to present itself in various forms in my office over the years. Most recently, in a very dysfunctional couple I was treating, the wife withheld sex and the husband complained about it endlessly. I asked the wife whether she was concerned that he might seek sex elsewhere. "He's a married man!" she exclaimed. "Really?" said I. "Are you familiar with the term extramarital relationships?" I pointed out that her husband was good looking, worked amongst many women at a major corporation, and that opportunities for assignations abounded. "Oh, he'd never stoop to that" she replied. Guess what? He ended up doing a lot more than stooping!

The "tinge of insecurity" to which I referred is a useful notion that does indeed generate a healthy respect for one another and prevents anyone from being taken too much for granted.

MYTH 8

Good Spouses Should Make Their Partners Happy

One of the most unfortunate errors that many people make is to accept and assume responsibility for other people's feelings. "It's my fault that Herman is unhappy. I just don't know how to be a good enough wife for him." "I would do anything to make Martha happy, but whatever I do seems to have the opposite effect."

The Happiness theme is an astonishing burden that many people place on themselves and others. Parents often feel guilty if their children are not happy, and children feel that they have let their parents down if they fail to make them proud and happy. The concept of "happiness," one's own or someone else's, is a standard that is often used to determine personal worth. One immediate problem is that the term "happiness" is rather vague. In some contexts, it implies the absence of pain, depression, anxiety, or other negative physical or emotional states. Here, we are told what to avoid, not what to seek. One of the major drawbacks to this idea of happiness is that emotional upsets, disappointments, and frustrations are an inevitable part of life. Attempting to escape the unavoidable can only intensify frustration, and may lead to self-blame and greater unhappiness. A misguided individual may imply: "Since I sometimes feel depressed, angry, or otherwise upset, it is obvious that you are delinquent in your duties as a spouse. If you were a good enough husband/wife, I wouldn't feel this way."

When happiness is defined as a state of contentment, fulfillment, or achievement, people often start wondering, "Am I really happy? Are other people happier than I am? If I am not happy, who is at fault?" Preoccupation with happiness often leads to unhappiness. The reality is that happiness will not be achieved when it is pursued directly. *Happiness is a byproduct of other activities.* The pursuit of happiness can only lead to frustration, if not unhappiness. Happy people have stopped focusing on themselves (or on trying to make somebody else happy) and instead, take responsibility for their own feelings and seek out enjoyable activities.

It has been said that happiness lies not in doing what you like but in liking what you do. The eminent statesman Disraeli stated that, "Action may not always bring happiness, but there is no happiness without action." Happiness is usually transitory; it is not a final and enduring state at which we can arrive. Benjamin Franklin stressed that "Human felicity is produced not so much by great pieces of good fortune that seldom happen, as by little advantages that occur every day." And Abraham Lincoln pointed out that "Most folks are about as happy as they make up their minds to be." These principles apply to marriage as well: it is not the responsibility of the partners to make each other happy. People are responsible for their own happiness or unhappiness.

Of course, the actions of others may place obstacles in one's path. It is easier to be happy around a loving, good humored, and supportive partner, than with one who is aggressive, spiteful, and hypercritical. But to say, "My spouse makes me unhappy with carping criticism" is psychologically inaccurate. For thousands of years, some philosophers have held that *we are not influenced or upset by events, but by our interpretation of events.* Thus, it would be more accurate to state: "I make *myself* unhappy over the fact that my husband puts me down in company," than "My husband upsets me by putting me down in company." We upset ourselves over other people's actions. It is not the actions per se that create the unhappiness.

Problems are inevitable when one looks to someone else for happiness. As I have emphasized, "preplanned" happiness tends to result in unexpected gloom. But if someone has the mind-set that happiness is in the hands of another, the tendency is to sit back, wait, and expect large portions of happiness to be dished up as if it were apple pie. The expectation that happiness will be manufactured or delivered by someone else creates a state of passivity or even lethargy — two definite factors that often lead to depression. Another confounding fact is that some people seem incapable of joy or happiness. The technical term is *anhedonia*, which is defined as the inability to derive pleasure or joy from experiences that most people find pleasurable. This brings to mind the case of Lionel and Jean.

For fifteen years, Jean ran herself ragged trying to make her beloved husband Lionel happy. She catered to his every whim. But Lionel remained unhappy. He said to me: "I wish that Jean were more stimulating, more exciting, more fun to be around." I inquired how stimulating, exciting, and how much fun it was to be around *him*. "That's beside the point," he said. "The trouble with Jean is that she is too easily satisfied. She's content to sit at home, to read a book, watch TV. I crave excitement." In truth, Lionel was a malcontent. He had a talent for finding fault with virtually everything and everyone (including himself). Yet Jean blamed herself and said if she were a better wife perhaps Lionel would be a happier man. It took years to convince Jean that it is impossible to *make* anyone happy, least of all Lionel, and that she would be doing herself and her husband a favor if she attended to her own happiness and allowed Lionel to do the same for himself. As Jean stopped taking responsibility for Lionel's happiness, she became more relaxed, more outgoing, and less anxious. When Lionel found that Jean no longer accepted the blame for everything that went wrong in his life, he started occupying his time more productively. He took skiing, tennis, and sailing lessons, joined a book club, and enrolled in an English literature course.

Taking charge of your own gratification and fulfillment increases the likelihood that life in general, and marriage in particular, will be enjoyable and rewarding. If someone else is placing obstacles in your path, some positive and assertive action is warranted. It is not up to your spouse (or anyone else) to make you happy, nor should you permit anyone to undermine whatever fun, joviality or buoyant feelings you can inject into your life.

MYTH 8 REVISITED

Betsy, a single 32-year-old woman said: "Being in a good marriage will enable me to be much happier than remaining unmarried." She was probably correct. But had she said that it is the duty of a good husband to make her happy, trouble would lie ahead. Not only would she be making the errors outlined in this chapter, but also one may well suspect that she saw marriage as a one-way street — its purpose was to enable *her* to be happy. "I want a soul mate to whom and for whom I can do nice things" is quite a different expectation. Better yet is the pledge: "I want a partner who will treat me with love, respect, kindness, tolerance, caring and concern, and to whom I will furnish the same."

The final sentence in this chapter captures the essential theme. It is not up to your spouse or anyone else to make you happy. But try not to allow anyone to undermine whatever fun and joy you can inject into your life.

MYTH 9

In Good Marriages, Husbands and Wives "Let It All Hang Out"

*B*ert finally agreed — very reluctantly — to pay me a visit. Valerie, his second wife for the past eight years, had already met with me three times to discuss her depression, her problems at work, and above all, her abuse at home. I had asked her to bring Bert in to tell me his side of the story.

After stressing that he was not "nuts," and that he had come to see me solely to assist Valerie with *her* hangups, Bert invited me to "fire away with any questions." I asked him about some of Valerie's claims: Was it true that he often yelled at Valerie, and in a fit of temper had punched a hole in the wall, thrown a color TV set through the window, and hit Valerie in the stomach? Had he really flung a cup of hot coffee at his 14-year-old stepson, fortunately missing the boy but staining the new wallpaper in the kitchen? Bert looked very matter-of-fact, shrugged his shoulders and said, "Well, you know how it is, Doc. If a man can't let down his hair at home and blow off some steam, he's likely to end up with stomach ulcers or have a heart attack."

Bert was expressing the sentiments of many who believe that home is the place where you can "let it all hang out." The workplace is seldom the proper milieu for full self-expression. At work, most people find it necessary to be on their best behavior, to display tact and diplomacy, to curb their tempers, and to think twice before reacting. Thus, home becomes a haven for spontaneity, the place to release the pent up emotions that accumulate in other settings. This mistaken idea can result in behaviors which have dire consequences.

I am by no means advocating an inhibited, excessively polite marital relationship. Spontaneity, sharing of fundamental feelings, openness, and informality are some of the most important elements of a satisfying marriage. But let there also be a sense of propriety and good taste. Marital freedom is not an invitation to attack each other's sense of dignity and self-esteem with emotional napalm.

Stella's temper could reach a frenetic pitch within seconds. It mattered little where she was, who was present, or what was going on at the time. When irked, she would unleash her shrill falsetto voice, while her face turned beet red with rage and her body trembled. Her angry words cut deeper than a stiletto knife. Stella's first marriage was annulled after two months — her husband had simply walked out and refused to return. Henry, her second husband (they had been married almost a year when he consulted me) had assumed that marriage would curb her temper. "I thought her main problem was that she'd had a bad marriage and then moved back home with her parents, and was just irritable and upset. I figured if she remarried and moved into her own home, she would calm down." But her temper had not abated, and her unbridled attacks, with Henry as the predominant target, had even intensified.

Since Henry was too afraid to ask Stella to set up an appointment with me, he and I composed a letter which prompted her to see me. She claimed that Henry exaggerated, that he came from such an uptight background that any expression of emotion was miscon-strued as a personal attack. I saw them together for a couple of sessions, and Stella's desire to have a child became the main topic of discussion. Henry said: "I refuse to bring a child into a home where it will be abused." Stella exploded! Although her tirade was uncontrolled — she had clearly *lost* her temper — her words were nevertheless carefully selected and pointedly aimed at Henry's heart and jugular. After she had calmed down, I endeavored to explore constructive alternatives. This fell on deaf ears. Stella accused me of being as uptight as Henry and claimed that her expression of anger was simply an "honest and spontaneous" reaction. Because her explosion was so out of proportion to the situation, I wondered if she perhaps had a hormonal or neurological imbalance, and tactfully tried to persuade her to consult the appropriate physicians. She refused to do so. The marriage endured for another few months; Henry then instituted divorce proceedings on grounds of "mental cruelty."

In certain Mediterranean and Latin American cultures, volatile, strongly expressive behaviors are the norm. Yelling, screaming, and other high decibel performances have a very different impact there than is true for most members of our society. There, it goes in one ear and out the other; here, it is perceived as an assault, as something to be reckoned with.

The wife of a prominent surgeon made a tape recording of one of their marital spats and brought the tape to her therapy session. I heard her husband deliver the following speech: "You are an ignorant fool. You come from a background of uneducated peasants and basically, you belong in the gutter. You are not only stupid, you are also evil. You are a rotten mother, you never should have had children. Whether you know it or not, everyone who meets you soon gets to despise you. I wish I could find one redeeming characteristic, but you have none. You're a frumpy, boring, dowdy little bitch and I wish that you would do me and the whole world a favor by dropping dead!"

What had provoked this intemperate outburst? She had questioned his judgement. The details are unimportant; the fact was that she had dared to insinuate that he had shown a lack of prudence and discretion toward a member of her family. As always, within a few hours, he grew exceedingly contrite, begged her forgiveness, and said he hadn't meant a word he had said.

I have seen mutually destructive battles in my office, between otherwise refined professional partners, that make some of the more explosive scenes from *Who's Afraid of Virginia Woolf* pale into insignificance. The vast majority had never allowed themselves to exhibit such behaviors to friends, colleagues, or even other family members (excluding children). Isn't it remarkable that people often treat perfect strangers with courtesy and kindness, yet they heap abuse on the people closest to them? I tell couples: "Treat your spouse with at least as much respect as you would afford a perfect stranger."

Displaced aggression is responsible for a large percentage of unhappy marriages and eventual divorces. Instead of tackling the source of their frustrations, many people reach a peak of unexpressed irritation, and then go home and kick their dogs, beat their children, and abuse their spouses. Many see nothing improper or shameful in so doing; after all, they were merely acting naturally, being themselves, letting off some steam!

Attacks generate counterattacks. People who resort to the aggressive maneuvers we have been discussing, usually get back in some form what they have been dishing out. The most common retaliation is "passive-aggressive" behavior, in which the injured party avoids open warfare. Rather than going toe-to-toe with the attacker, this person goes underground and becomes a saboteur.

Nora, for example, felt extremely angry when Marv lost his temper or was overly critical of her, but she would never oppose him directly. After one of his typical outbursts, she "accidentally" burned his dinner, "lost" a cigarette lighter to which he was sentimentally attached, "forgot" to pick up his shirts from the laundry, and managed to get back at him in three or four other indirect ways. One way or another, most people end up paying for their aggressive behavior.

Another myth that relates very closely to the points I have been making is: *A good marriage is based on unconditional positive regard.* One often hears the refrain that people want to be loved for themselves. They seek an unrealistic degree of attachment and devotion as if they were utterly irresistible — even when they behave abominably. *True* love, as some would have it, is not in response to one's sense of humor, charm, caring, or consideration. These folks expect to be loved when these pleasant accouterments are conspicuously absent, when one gives the other person nothing but grief. In the minds of these deluded souls, that proves that one is indeed loved for one's "self."

People who endorse such unfortunate ideas (and they are far less rare than one might suppose) push their partners to the breaking point. They test the limits in the hopes of finding infinite enchantment. They never find what they seek, for love and positive regard are reciprocal and conditional.

Intimate relationships require the same courtesy, civility, and respect that we are apt to pay to total strangers. Politeness, tact, good humor, and pleasing behavior all help to create a relaxed and loving home atmosphere. And these factors are under our control. We decide whether to be kind or unkind, even-tempered or irascible. The path of wrath almost invariably exacts a steep price.

Another popular myth related to this area of relationships is that *True love means never having to say you are sorry.* In truth, unless husband and wife are each willing to acknowledge being wrong and are ready to apologize for their errors or lack of consideration, their marriage will be characterized by resentment, tension, and even hatred. If you've done something for which you're sorry, by all means say so.

MYTH 9 REVISITED

Most authorities agree that a successful relationship requires the couple to have a high level of basic compatibility and agreement as exemplified by similar tastes in mundane matters (e.g. food, movies, furniture, music) and harmony vis-a-vis important ideological and personal issues (e.g., sex, ethical standards, expectations, attitudes and beliefs.) At a clinical meeting where these issues were under discussion, a seasoned therapist self-disclosed that his first marriage, despite the presence of all the compatibility criteria, ended in divorce after a couple of years. They had enjoyed a high level of intellectual compatibility, both loved the theater, enjoyed the same kinds of music, were politically in accord, had the same religious outlook, similar tastes in food, wine, people, recreational activities, sports and hobbies. Their sex life was exciting and gratifying. So what could possibly have gone wrong?

The doctor claimed that his ex-wife had a vicious and violent temper that was easily triggered by minor events. She exploded with rage and often behaved "like the Tasmanian Devil and would go ballistic at unexpected moments." He had seen her unleash her temper at her parents and siblings, but he only became the target of her full fury several months into the marriage. A course of therapy, both medical and psychological, was unsuccessful. Despite all her charm and other positive attributes, he was unwilling to be subjected to her rage and fury for the rest of his life, and he sued for divorce. The moral of the story from his perspective is that mood, disposition, and temperament are the most important variables, and that the first attribute to look for in a potential mate is sweetness and light.

- It can be argued that temperamental compatibility is more important than compatibility of interests and taste. Flying off the handle makes holes in the marital boat. Do it enough times, and you will surely take on enough water to sink to the bottom.

Good Husbands Do Household Repairs; Good Wives Do the Laundry

his myth is almost exclusively American in character. Our emphasis on do-it-yourself and fix-it-yourself plays a significant role in what I am about to describe, as does a lingering prejudice that there are exclusively male and female household duties. Many believe that a spouse who neglects to play the proper part at the correct time and in the right way is delinquent in his or her marital obligations.

There is much talk today about equal rights, the collapse of rigid sex stereotypes, and the emphasis on individuality. Nevertheless, I am sure that if we had a hidden camera monitoring the activities of husbands and wives in every home, we would still find mostly men, and few women, wielding the power tools, hammers and nails, hacksaws, lathes, crowbars, wrenches, screwdrivers, and similar paraphernalia. Conversely, many of these tool-brandishing males, when asked to run a load of laundry, probably gawk at the washing machine as if it were some alien device about to explode.

If my point is somewhat overstated, some of the following case histories will nonetheless show how marital distress often comes from clearcut his-and-hers household expectations and demarcations.

Let's start with Matthew, a 35-year-old attorney, very macho, very successful, somewhat rigid, and very cheap. Before law school, Matthew graduated from college as a mechanical engineer. A very handy fellow, he could take a car to pieces and put it back together again. With all due immodesty, he openly claimed that he could fix just about anything. He complained about the incompetence of carpenters, electricians, plumbers, and auto mechanics. "If you want it done right, you have to do it yourself!" A difficult man to please, he was so critical and opinionated that Janet, his 30-year-old wife, had threatened to leave unless he agreed to marriage therapy (which is how I got into the act).

Matthew and Janet lived in a home that they both described as "magnificent." Despite the splendor, a large hole in the living room ceiling, caused in turn by a leak in the roof, called for a bucket in the center of the room whenever it rained (to protect a valuable Persian rug). This situation had existed for over three months. To call in outsiders to repair the broken shingles, and to repair, plaster, and paint the ceiling was unthinkable; Matthew insisted on doing it himself. Trees in the garden needed pruning, hedges needed cutting and shaping. Call in a gardener? Never! Matthew would attend to it. Matthew's law practice was booming, and all of his spare time was devoted to refurbishing an antique car that he planned to sell for a substantial profit. "Meanwhile," Janet explained, "every day of my life I see that hole in the ceiling. As I look into the garden, I see all the weeds, the misshaped hedges, dead branches in the trees; and as I drive in and out of the garage, I see the side of the house with all the paint peeling off."

"How about giving Matthew one month to get everything on track," I suggested. "If by that time there are still outstanding matters that need attention, Janet, you are free to call in whomsoever you please. Is that fair enough, Matthew?" He tried to bargain for six weeks, but Janet said that even a month seemed too generous; Matthew begrudgingly agreed. I typed up what we psychologists call a *contingency contract* for Matthew's signature: "I hereby agree that after one month's time, unless the hole in the living room ceiling has been repaired, the outside of the house has been painted, the trees, hedges and shrubs have been attended to, Janet has my full permission to call in the necessary work force, for which she will receive no argument and for which I shall pay in full." Matthew read the agreement with an attorney's skepticism, grimaced, then signed and dated it.

Matthew managed to hold up his end of the bargain, except for the gardening. Janet accordingly contacted a service that sent out men who had everything shipshape in a day. Clearly, this had no impact on Matthew's penchant to undertake far too many "masculine chores," but thereafter, Janet came up with her own contingency contracts which she had Matthew sign and uphold.

The situation between Keith and Avril was quite different. Keith was responsible for more than fifty people at his place of work, and put in long hours. On weekends, he wanted nothing more than to relax and spend time with Avril and their four-year-old son. Avril had taught English and mathematics at a junior high school, but after her son was born, elected to be a full-time housewife and mother. In her book, a good husband was not one who sat around relaxing and watching television on weekends. There was plenty of work to be done around the house. A "good wife" reminded her husband of the chores that required attention. It was not unusual for Keith to be presented with a list of forty items which Avril expected him to complete before Monday morning!

Unlike Matthew, Keith was more than willing to pay someone else to perform the household services. "I can well afford it," he said, "and whatever it would cost would be worth it. I work hard enough during the week. I feel entitled to some rest and relaxation on weekends." Avril strongly disagreed, insisting that "a man should show some pride and interest in his house, and unless he attends to things himself, how can he really appreciate it?" She added: "My dad had a motto: 'Never call an outsider to do an insider's job.' It's Keith's responsibility to do the manly things around the house. I'm not asking him to cook or do the laundry."

I tried, to no avail, to persuade her to modify her rigid thinking. The discussion then focused on the grass in their back yard which Keith mowed on Sunday mornings. When the grass had been cut, Avril would invariably find fault with Keith's performance. The edges were not straight, or he had left a zig-zag pattern in the middle, or some other criticism would be levelled. I asked the obvious question: "Avril, why don't you cut the grass yourself?" She threw a withering look at me and flatly declared: "That's not my job!"

Sad to say, I made no headway with this couple. I expect they're still arguing over "whose job it is!"

Taking out the garbage seems to be primarily a masculine prerogative. I recall a couple for whom that simple chore served as the center of a tremendous power struggle. Corrine felt strongly that this was something her husband should do to "pull his weight around the house." Tim did not object but insisted on doing it in his own time. Corrine, a fastidious individual, felt that the trash should be transferred to the outside garbage cans as soon as the inside receptacle was full. Typically, she would carry the garbage herself as far as the outside door. She was unwilling to walk the extra ten feet to get the garbage out of the house. On several occasions, while Tim and Corrine locked horns, the garbage stayed in the den, propped up against the outside door for more than three days!

Another couple made a portable window air conditioner their battering ram. Their west-facing bedroom was like a sauna in the summer. Day after day, week after week, Elsie pleaded with Charles to take the air conditioner down from the attic (where it had been stored for the winter) and install it in the bedroom. Time passed, and the couple sweltered. Charles did not get around to putting in the air conditioner, yet refused to have someone come in and take the burden off his hands. After all, why pay someone to do something that he was perfectly capable of doing himself?

All these cases are more complex, of course, but this is not the place to go into the hidden agendas and underlying dynamics. Suffice it to say that if I agree to clean the windows, and do not get around to doing so, or do a slipshod job, I open myself to justifiable criticism. But if I make it clear from the start that I don't do windows, and my partner chooses to enter a relationship with me on those terms, I'm not responsible, even if the windows become too filthy to allow in any light.

Me? Well, I have made it very clear that I am not a plumber, or a carpenter, or an electrician, or a builder, or a mechanic, or a gardener. But I have been known to change a light bulb, and on occasion, I do take out the garbage.

MYTH 10 REVISITED

Rigid masculine and feminine role demarcations seem to have receded considerably over the years. Fewer couples these days seem to haggle over whose job it is to perform certain chores. Nevertheless, many of the case scenarios described in this chapter are still enacted. The main complaint seems to be that requests are not carried out in good time. Thus, Meryl agrees to help Max with the income tax returns, but he wants her assistance right now and she first wants to attend to some other matters. Bonnie wants her husband to replant a shrub when he gets home from work, but he refuses to get to it before the weekend. I advise couples to discuss time constraints and to accept the fact that it is just fine for items and issues to receive attention outside their own preferred time frame. If the interval begins to lag beyond what seems fair and fitting, the use of contingency contracts, a la Matthew and Janet, might well be considered.

Most recently, with a professional couple I was seeing, let's call them Nelson and Grace, the bone of contention revolved around air conditioning, much like Elsie and Charles. In the case of Nelson and Grace, however, it was not a window unit that needed to be installed. They had several inefficient and noisy window units, and Grace wanted central air conditioning. Nelson was too cheap. These minor points of disagreement can wreak havoc on a marriage. Resentments mount on both sides and can often begin to unravel a relationship.

It is advisable for couples to work in tandem, to avoid power struggles, to studiously avoid making unfair demands, and to agree to help each other promptly and pleasantly with tasks, chores, and other household responsibilities. The entire transaction gets soured when you do good deeds for your spouse begrudgingly.

MYTH 11

Having a Child Will Improve a Bad Marriage

*I*n general, children tend to consolidate and enhance a good marriage. In a bad marriage, this extra burden usually serves to make things worse.

Most people will admit that being a good parent is not easy. The responsibilities of good parenting are enormous. The advent of a child can bring to light hidden conflicts and significant differences of opinion in couples who had previously functioned harmoniously. If marital harmony is to prevail, husband and wife must agree on such matters as care and discipline of children, their education, the location of the home, allocation of various items in the family budget, and similar personal and interpersonal matters.

Distressed or unhappy couples are often characterized by a conflict between the partners' personal ambitions and the welfare of the family. I have seen many a father, for instance, who would never deny himself an expensive car, yet who refused to feed or clothe his family adequately. Society says, "Be an individual," and "Live your own life." Those ideas are often in conflict with putting family first, and taking care of self-interest only *after* the needs of the family have been met.

The sociologists who study such phenomena have suggested that the majority of families "muddle through." Most people seem to regard tension, arguments, and unpleasantness as both normal and inevitable. In fact some have declared that if family members *don't* clash with each other, and don't have an occasional brawl or melee, something must be seriously wrong. Nonharmonious functioning is, alas, held up as the norm!

Occasional brief and petty quarrels are indeed "normal" enough and are not grounds for concern. Certainly, when first married, some clashes may be expected. Initial adjustments and constant readjustments are necessary for two unique people from different homes to learn to live together harmoniously. Rifts between husband and wife can harden into permanent friction, however, unless steps are taken to remedy the situation (such as seeking professional counseling.)

Is there really much chance that tension between husband and wife is likely to be dissipated by the birth, or adoption of a baby? Temporarily, the infant may serve to distract the parents. But the unheeded tensions will surely surface sooner or later with the added burden of caring for a totally dependent being. Celia and Frank are a case in point. Their relationship was somewhat stormy from the start. Despite frequent heated arguments, they decided to get married. Why? "Although we fought like cat and dog, we loved each other and thought that once we were married, things would get better," explained Celia. Wrong! Therein lies yet another myth. Instead of improving matters, they found that marriage imposed additional demands and obligations. They had even resorted to physical violence on occasion. They came to me for help at a point where they were feuding almost constantly.

Their problems seemed to stem from their early family experiences. Frank, for example, saw in Celia some of the attributes he'd been fighting in his mother ever since his parents' divorce when he was eleven years old. He described his mother as a "harsh disciplinarian," and over-reacted when Celia expressed any discontent. Moreover, Frank had felt unloved by his mother, and his need for affection was extreme. Celia, in turn, had learned to be independent at a young age. Her parents were both alcoholics, and she had to fend for herself and protect her brother, six years her junior. But her psychic scars were such that if Frank touched hard liquor, or drank more than a couple of beers, she became belligerent.

We had no sooner started working on these and other problems in therapy, when Celia announced that she was pregnant. Frank urged her to have an abortion, but Celia insisted on having the child, stating that she was sure this would solve their problems and solidify the marriage. Frank asked for my opinion. I stated my view that the time to have a child is when a marriage is sound rather than unsound. Celia refused to terminate the pregnancy.

I continued seeing the couple, and we made some headway concerning their misunderstandings and hypersensitivities. Celia gave birth to a daughter, and I did not see them again until the baby was three months old. "Things are terrible!" Celia exclaimed. Frank agreed: "That's putting it mildly." One key problem was that the baby disturbed their sleep — "I walk around in a fog all day," Frank declared. Even more important, Frank's insatiable need for affection was seriously compromised. "He resents the time I spend with the baby," explained Celia. She added: "I feel that I have *two* babies to attend to. Frank is jealous of his own child!" My attempts to help the couple resolve their problems and establish a positive relationship were unsuccessful. Their marriage ended in an acrimonious divorce. Perhaps this union was ill-fated from the start and no amount of counseling or therapy would have had an enduring benefit. Had the couple not complicated matters by having a child so soon, however, I think the marriage might have been saved.

In the past, a woman's role was largely determined by her status as a child-bearer. The modern woman's reasons for entering marriage have shifted, and her revolt against subservience has gained considerable ground. Men and women of today are governed by a sense of individualism. Yet successful parenting calls for husbands and wives to willingly sacrifice many of their own egotistic desires. Harmonious family functioning calls for a "we," in place of an "I," point of view. The advent of a baby is a point of crisis that places new demands on a marriage. If the couple has built up habits and responses that are inadequate for the new situation, family disintegration is virtually inevitable.

MYTH 11 REVISITED

Research suggests that children from broken homes do not fare as well as those from intact homes. This has been used by some to recommend that even if a marriage is intolerably tense the children will be better off if the parents stay together. I think much more detailed research is called for to resolve this issue, but my clinical findings still lead me to believe that kids are usually better off with divorced parents than in a home where both parents feel miserable and act maliciously toward one another. Of course, children are fortunate if their parents are able to achieve an amicable divorce and do not put them in the middle of a war zone.

Just today I saw a couple whose level of compatibility is almost zero. This marriage should never have taken place. The wife believes that a child will remedy matters! She was totally unresponsive to my counter-arguments and I shudder at the thought that yet another innocent being may have to suffer the consequences of being raised in an atmosphere of extreme derangement.

Having a child is an enormous responsibility and inevitably imposes a strain and new pressures on a marriage. If a marriage is not stable and harmonious, having a child will only make matters worse. It is an act of cruelty to bring a child into a tense and faltering marital situation. A child is not a throwaway plaything.

MYTH 12

Marriage Should be a 50-50 Partnership

*E*qual rights, equal opportunities, equal pay, and equal time have become catchwords. Equality and democracy are viewed by many as synonymous and highly desirable. Unless things are shared equally — divided right down the middle — it is assumed that exploitation will result. Egalitarianism becomes equated with freedom. In enlightened circles, the "lord of the castle" no longer calls for his pipe, his slippers, and his drink. The urbane male of today is likely to be slaving over a hot stove (or, more realistically, pushing buttons on a microwave oven) while his executive wife relaxes in the living room with a drink and the stock market reports.

The weakening of rigid male-female roles and fixed stereotypes of masculine and feminine functions probably reflects genuine progress and enlightenment. However, misapplication of the idea of 50-50 divisions, and the notion that joint participation is necessarily fair and desirable, has led many marriages astray. The point that some couples overlook is that while people may be *equal* to one another, they also *differ* from each other. Thus, under given circumstances, 60-40, 70-30, 75-25, or any other combination may be far better than 50-50.

Here are some cases in point:

Harold prided himself on being a feminist, and he was quick to notice even tacit hints of male chauvinism in himself and in others. When he married Marge, he insisted that they divide all household chores down the middle. "After all, we both work, we earn equal money, we both come home tired, so I'll fix dinner one night and you do the cooking the next night." On the face of it, there seemed little wrong with Harold's proposal. What could be fairer? But Harold forgot to factor in one significant reality. He was a lousy cook! Not only were his best-intended concoctions often inedible, but the time and hard labor that went into his preparation of even the simplest meals (not to mention the waste!) rendered Harold's 50-50 idea excessively cost-ineffective. All the more so since Marge loved cooking and had the talent for whipping up exciting, nutritious, and delicious meals with hardly any effort. Clearly, Harold had not taken into account some key factors in their specific relationship.

Ken and Jodi ran into a different problem. Their four-month-old baby was not a good sleeper. Little Lisa needed to be fed and changed at least twice during the night. It seemed eminently fair in Jodi's mind for Ken and her to take equal turns attending to Lisa. They both worked hard. Jodi was a caseworker at a community mental health center. She often found her work tedious and demanding. "I work just as hard as Ken, so it's only fair that he get up for Lisa one night and I attend to her the next night." Thus, Jodi was proposing the same 50-50 division of labor that Harold had come up with. Of course, the case of Harold's low C.Q. (Culinary Quotient) versus Marge's genius C.Q. cannot be equated to Ken and Jodi's situation — Ken was no less capable than Jodi of changing diapers and holding a baby bottle!

Ken had his own side of the story: "I'm usually at the hospital scrubbing on a case at 7:15 a.m., and unless I get a good six or seven hours of solid sleep, I feel foggy and uncoordinated." (I made a mental note to ask my surgeon, if I am scheduled for an operation, to be sure to get a good night's sleep before cutting me open!) Jodi considered this a "cop out" and asserted that her work was just as important and just as taxing as Ken's. I argued while the work of a surgeon may be no more important than that of a caseworker, it certainly is more exacting. "He's got life and death in his hands," I protested, "and if his mind is fogged up and he feels uncoordinated because he was up tending to the baby, his hand could slip."

The solutions for these two couples were relatively simple. Marge did all the cooking, but Harold did all the food shopping. Jodi attended to the baby five nights, and Ken got up for Lisa Friday and Saturday; Ken willingly took care of the household laundry — washing, drying, sorting and packing. For these couples, unequal trade-offs promoted a sense of balance and harmony.

There are many couples who take on decidedly unequal tasks simply because they prefer it that way. I have a good friend, an accountant and a gourmet cook, who shoulders nearly all of the household responsibilities. He waits on his wife, and has perhaps a 90-10 partnership vis-a-vis the running of the home. That's the way *he and his wife* want it, and it works for them. Conversely, I know couples who have a "traditional" marriage in which the wives cook, do all the cleaning, the laundry, all the marketing. There is more than one right way for couples to deal with each other. The marriage dyad is an intricate system — what truly satisfies one couple and yields genuine love, caring and respect, could be completely destructive for another.

Sally-Anne emphasized that she loved being a homemaker. Andy put in a hard day's work as the breadwinner, and when he came home, she enjoyed attending to his creature comforts. "Some women have come right out and said that I am the victim of brainwashing, that I need to attend consciousness-raising groups to become an adult. I think an adult is someone who makes her own choices, and this is *my* choice, at least for now." Unfortunately too many people insist that there is only one right way to view the world, usually their *own* way.

I am often amused by couples who keep score cards. "I cooked five meals to your two. I took out the garbage four times to your three. I did two loads of laundry to your one. I vacuumed the rug in the living room six times to your one half-hearted effort." I have, on occasion, asked clients to keep short-term "logs" as a means of increasing their awareness of what's going on in the relationship.

But a need to prove "how much harder I'm working than you are" seems to me to signal a basic lack of love, of genuine concern, of deep commitment.

When you truly love someone, you enjoy doing things for that person; it is a pleasure, if not a delight, to be able to make life a little easier and more pleasant for him or her. Thus, when I see husbands or wives waving their tally sheets, counting points, shouting "You owe me!" I sadly realize that sooner or later, they will probably be employing divorce lawyers.

MYTH 12 REVISITED

I don't think I can add anything significant here. The major theme is that "equal" does not always add up to 50-50 and those couples who keep score are likely to make some divorce lawyer even richer.

The importance of reciprocity in a marriage is a given. The partners help one another and are both enriched for it. What may look like inequality or even exploitation to an outsider may feel just fine to the couple under scrutiny. I typically ask couples "is your spouse pulling his or her weight?" If the answer is affirmative I do not waste time second-guessing them. If there is dissention, we revert to each person's expectations and see if we can level the playing field.

MYTH 13

Marriage Can Fulfill All Your Dreams

*E*ven in this age of enlightenment and emancipation, there are many people who consider marriage a crowning achieve- ament, a notable sign of success. To be married carries a special status in the minds of these individuals. It proves their basic worth; it shows the world that somebody wanted them enough to "tie the knot." These sentiments, because of social conditioning, are probably held more often by women than by men. The term "bachelor" does not have the same demeaning undertones as "spinster" or "old maid." Nevertheless, some men also fall prey to the myth that marriage can fulfill all their dreams. One wag has observed: "No woman ever reaches thirty without having been asked to marry — at least by her parents." (Despite our considerable progress toward equality, parents still seem *much* more concerned about their daughters marrying than about their sons.)

Betty espoused views that are typical of many women who have consulted me because of low self-esteem. She described herself as "a loser." Attractive and well-groomed, she had many women friends and several men who were her "pals," but since her divorce six years ago, there had been no meaningful man in her life. At 39, Betty held a highly responsible, well-paid executive position, and was being groomed for a company rank occupied by fewer than 5% — men or women. But in her own eyes, none of this meant anything. She irrationally blamed herself for the failure of her marriage and, far worse, in six years she had not developed an enduring relationship with anyone she considered suitable for remarriage. Thus, in her eyes, her other achievements amounted to zero. Because she had not remarried, she considered herself "a nobody."

Lynn, age 35, had similar problems of low self-esteem. Unlike Betty, she was married and had two children. "All my life," she said, "I was groomed to be a wife and mother. My entire childhood was shaped in that direction. I learned needlework, sewing, cooking, and baking. After high school, I selected a college not for its academic ranking, but for its reputation as a social meeting ground. My sole purpose for attending college was to find a husband, and find one I did. Joe and I were married as soon as we both graduated." Now, some thirteen years into the marriage, with sons twelve and ten, Lynn had satisfied her script. "We even have a white picket fence, a station wagon, and a dog — no kidding!" But instead of experiencing fulfillment of her lifelong dreams, Lynn had noticed restive feelings entering into her life. "They crept in slowly at first, and then I began to allow myself to ask if this is really all there is to life!"

Fran was especially bewildered. Her history and background were very similar to Lynn's, but at 42 she was the familiar victim of "a younger woman." Her husband had become involved with one of his secretaries and had left Fran eight months ago. "I have been programmed to be a wife," she said, "and that's all I know." Here again, marriage was supposed to fulfill all her dreams. "It's all I ever wanted; I was perfectly happy."

Betty, Lynn, and Fran are in different predicaments, but all three are victims of the "marriage as the be-all and end-all" mythology. What help is there for the Bettys, Lynns, and Frans of this world? The solution lies in enabling them to develop a well-rounded outlook, in which marriage is only one ingredient (and not absolutely essential) for a happy and fulfilled life.

A wide variety of interpersonal skills is necessary if one is to develop into a well-adjusted person. Sympathy, genuine affection, the capacity for friendship and companionship are necessities for enduring positive relationships. Sexual skills are an important part of self-esteem and self-confidence. (The idea that, *if love is present, good sex will inevitably prevail,* is yet another myth. See Myth 23.) Sexual skills must be learned; love is not enough. But sexual prowess and proficiency are also not enough to promote sustained love relationships. Work and other outside responsibilities and stimulation can prevent domestic burnout. True, there are men and women who find gratification in full-time domesticity. There is nothing wrong in being a "homebody," except when it renders one vulnerable in the face of family disruption, as with Fran.

How many slim, attractive, well-groomed people have, almost immediately after marriage, let themselves go, and become overweight, sloppy, and to say the least, unpleasant? Prior to marriage, they expended effort and put their best foot forward. The goal? To capture the unsuspecting victim. Once the marriage license had duly been signed, it was "unnecessary" to exert any more effort. How sad!

The marriage-as-total-fulfillment fallacy is clearly related to myth number two (romantic love) but has some distinctive features. When one makes marriage a *sine qua non* for life itself, emotional blackmail is a frequent occurrence. "I can't live without you. If you leave me, I'll kill myself!" Too many of these marriages remain glued together, not by love, caring, or happiness, but through guilt and fear. The spouse becomes transformed into the partner's "emotional oxygen," without which life cannot be sustained. Such people tell their mates, "You mean everything to me; you are my whole universe." This unhealthy dependency fosters resentment — on both parts. The dependent partner resents his or her "savior" for being indispensable, while the "stronger" person feels trapped, angry, and often anxious. Such marriages are referred to as "symbiotic attachments," which implies that one person is depending on another for the satisfaction of neurotic desires, for exploitation rather than for cooperative support and affection.

Mature love never transforms the other person into "emotional oxygen." A mature person's message is: "I can live with or without you. I much prefer to live with you because I love you. I hope that you feel the same way about me." Immature attachments lead to a very different statement. "You are mine and I'll never let you go." In these instances, "emotional blackmail" and similar power tactics are not uncommon. Consider the following dialogue:

Quinn: I don't think that we are suited to each other. I've given it a lot of thought, and the conclusion I've arrived at is that we'd both be better off if we got divorced.

Lydia: If you ask for a divorce again, I'll tell your mother about your affair with Gladys, and about the money you embezzled.

Quinn: (Stunned) Why would you do that? My mother has always been kind to you. You know that she couldn't handle something like that. Why would you want to hurt my mother?

Lydia: Just don't go getting any funny ideas!

To keep someone trapped in a loveless marriage is not a good idea! Yet many people for whom marriage is everything insist on remaining in the relationship, despite the knowledge that they are not really desired, loved, or respected by their spouses. Such marriage-as-an-end-in-itself relationships usually lack mutual happiness, healthy togetherness, love, kindness, genuine caring, and joy.

A good marriage is one highly important, desirable component of a fulfilling life, but not absolutely essential. The view that marriage in and of itself is *everything* is a false conception that can bring only pain and disillusionment.

MYTH 13 REVISITED

In today's world, terms like "spinster" and "old maid" are pretty much passe and are regarded as sexist and politically incorrect. In addition, there is no longer a stigma to being single – regardless of gender – and single parenthood has become far more prevalent. Career women had certainly entered the work scene in 1985 when *Marital Myths* was published, but in today's corporate world and marketplace, the number of women in top executive positions has increased. Nevertheless, all the scenarios described in this myth have by no means disappeared. But in the last few years, I have seen many more women who are stressed out by top-drawer work demands than those who share Betty's plight. The dilemmas described by Lynn and Fran are still very much in evidence. And symbiotic attachments and emotional blackmail, as exemplified in the dialogue between Quinn and Lydia, are anything but rare.

- Post-marital misery and the high divorce rate would probably be reduced if people entered marriage fully knowing what it entails. It is not smart to get married because of peer or parental pressure. And it is most unwise to ignore any sense you may have beforehand that the relationship will not work. Your gut can often override your heart in telling your head what to do! Even if you have no premarital doubts or jitters, some intelligent counseling and guidance might save you an enormous amount of pain in the long run.

MYTH 14

True Lovers Automatically Know Each Other's Thoughts and Feelings

*T*his is another belief related to the romantic fallacy (Myth 2). Notions abound in which true compatibility involves "being of one mind," or "on the same wave length." Words are superfluous. As the pulp magazines so often put it: "Their eyes met across the room, and instantly they both *knew* what the other was thinking and feeling." True love gives one the powers of telepathy!

As is true for each of the marital myths, there is some grain of truth that has become magnified into the whole truth. Good friends, lovers, spouses, even work associates do best when each person understands the other to some degree, and is sensitive to the other's feelings, opinions, and preferences. Thus, one might learn to read one another's reactions quite accurately. "I caught the glint in your eye when Charlie was going on about his latest conquest and I realized that unless I got him out of the room, he would end up with a bloody nose." "I knew exactly what you were thinking when Grace started talking about that week in Mexico."

Nevertheless, one is also likely to misread another's thoughts and feelings. A typical dialogue:

Adam: Why are you angry?

Sue: I'm not angry. What makes you think I'm angry?

Adam: Oh yes you are. You can't fool me. I can tell when you're angry.

Sue: No, really. I'm not angry. I'll swear to it.

Adam: Who do you think you're fooling? Come clean! Own up to your feelings. Stop lying!

Sue: (Beginning to feel angry) I'm not lying to you! I'm telling you I'm not angry.

Adam: Then why are you raising your voice? Come on, own up to your feelings. I can read you like a book.

Sue: Look, I hate it when you start questioning my honesty. That makes me angry.

Adam: Aha! So you admit that you're angry!

Variations of the foregoing theme are almost endless. I have seen this scenario enacted between friends, lovers, spouses, enemies, and between therapists and their patients. The theme, "I know you better than you know yourself" is nonsense. Certainly, people are capable of fooling themselves, of disowning certain elements that objective outsiders may see through, but on the whole, nobody knows anyone else better than they know themselves. There are no mind readers! The preceding dialogue would be inoffensive if, instead of saying "Why are you angry?" Adam had inquired "Are you angry?" or had stated "You seem angry." Unless he had very good evidence, definite and clearcut facts that negated Sue's denials, Adam should have given at least the benefit of the doubt to her statement that she was not feeling angry. Instead, he was guilty of *mind raping.* Here is a basic rule: *Never tell someone else what he or she is thinking or feeling.*

How often I have heard people claim: "I shouldn't have to explain it to him! If he *truly* loved me, he would know it without being told." "My partner should know what I want. If I have to tell, then it's no good."

This unfortunate myth is especially prevalent in the area of sexual intimacy. "If I have to tell my husband how I like him to behave in bed, it takes away all the pleasure. Besides, if he really loved me, was tuned into me, it would be unnecessary to tell him what to do. He would just know." "When a woman is really in love with a man, she can sense exactly how to please and satisfy him. If she has to be shown how to turn him on, or told what and what not to do, she is not for him — and vice versa."

Poppycock! Human beings are the only animals that can communicate through spoken language. No other species is capable of saying: "Darling, will you put your hand there and press a little harder while rubbing my back with your other hand?" One can't experience another person's feelings, regardless of the intensity of one's devotion. People are not like insects that have a complex pattern of responses based on instinct. Human beings have to learn all complex behaviors (and gratifying sexual relations fall into this category!). We are born with some basic drives (e.g., hunger, thirst) and several reflexes (e.g., sucking, swallowing, breathing) but everything else is learned, acquired through instruction, by example, or by trial-and-error.

Of course, there are insensitive, uncaring people who can be told, shown, or taught over and over again to no good effect. "It really bothers me when you leave hairs all over the sink after shaving," or "I wish you wouldn't block my car in the driveway," or other explicit requests are simply disregarded. Such belligerence is perhaps part of yet another myth — "Don't let your spouse push you around. Show who is the boss!" Power struggles in marriage tend to lead to a fight to the death in divorce!

It certainly is rewarding to be able to predict the way a loved one will respond to a given event — and then to do or not do something, so that the end result is pleasant for both partners. "How did you know that I was wishing for a cassette player?" "It was very kind of you to realize that I would want to visit my aunt in the hospital, and to leave the office party early to bring the car home for me."

If each act of concern or consideration, each gesture of caring, every act of generosity must be explicitly coaxed out of one's partner, the quality of the alliance is undermined.

But the converse is also dangerous. "If you really loved me, or truly cared for me, you would have done *this*, or not done *that*, or thought of doing *the other thing.*" Beware of this type of reasoning! Instead, tell your partner, "When you do X −,or don't do Y −, I feel unloved." When expressing a gripe, instead of telling the other person why he or she performed the action that displeased you ("You did that to deliberately hurt me!"), the following format is strongly recommended:

"When you do X −,

in situation Y −

I feel Z −."

For example: "When you call my sister stupid and dumb, while we're visiting my parents, I feel embarrassed and sorry for her, and I feel annoyed with you for putting her down."

It makes sense for marriage partners to teach one another how best to get along with each other. This precludes mind-raping, second guessing, and all other tactics that diminish the significance of what someone is expressing. Say what you mean, mean what you say, and don't expect your spouse to read your mind.

MYTH 14 REVISITED

The false notion still persists in many quarters that "true love" will guide one quite automatically toward an intuitive knowledge of how to satisfy one's partner sexually. Similarly, "mind reading" remains a frequent and common habit.

- I can simply reiterate that couples need to be willing to fully discuss how best to satisfy each other sexually. It is particularly important not to mind read and never to tell anyone what he or she is feeling or thinking.

MYTH 15

An Unhappy Marriage Is Better than a Broken Home

There are few things more unpleasant than a loveless marriage held together by fear, guilt, or duty. I have seen the outcome of empty, hollow marriages that endured only because of social pressure, obligation, or "the sake of the children." I have a saying: "When it is for the sake of the children, the children will be forsaken!" When children are the basic glue that binds a marriage, their emotional needs are usually neglected. A home that exists in the absence of cooperation, without a community of interests, amounts to a sham imposed by social hypocrisy.

Many people continue to live under the same roof because of religious convictions that forbid divorce. Some women put up with endless friction, abuse, tension, and downright misery for economic reasons. Living with a husband whom she despises may be difficult, but it may be even harder for her to find gainful employment without experience or training beyond that of a housewife. Often, she rationalizes that she must remain there to protect the children.

David, a thirty-year-old computer programmer, had consulted me for help with his anxiety, depression, and sexual problems. He was fine during casual sex, but as soon as a relationship grew "serious," he would be impotent. His story was typical of hundreds of case histories I have heard over the years: "One of my earliest memories is that of my mother and father yelling at each other. You can't imagine how many nights I was awakened by their shouting and screaming. It used to terrify me. It was horrible! My dad usually took out his frustration on us kids, and my mom walked around looking so unhappy, so miserable. When I was nine or ten I asked her why she didn't get a divorce. As the saying goes, "At first I was afraid that my parents would separate, and then I was afraid that they wouldn't!' Later, she let us know that she had endured the marriage for our sakes. I wish she hadn't. I'm sure that my brother, my sister, and I would all have been happier in the long run if my parents would have split up. Two of my friends parents' were divorced. I loved sleeping over at their homes. One lived with his father and stepmother and everyone got along pretty well. The other lived with his mother and younger sister and we had a lot of fun together. I never brought my friends home. I was too ashamed and too uptight that mom and dad would start arguing."

Rhonda consulted me for help with a variety of emotional problems: "I'm here because my parents stayed together for my sake. If they hadn't, I doubt if I would need to see a shrink!" Unlike David's family, her parents kept their tensions hidden. "There were no ugly flareups; just a cold, uncaring, Arctic climate devoid of any warmth." Rhonda's parents finally did get divorced when she was twenty years old. "It came about ten to fifteen years too late as far as I was concerned.... In retrospect, I realize how profoundly my parents hated each other, but they maintained an impeccable outward shell for the community. Their friends regarded them as an ideal couple and often held them up as an example of marital bliss. Most people who knew them socially were absolutely dumbfounded, totally shocked, when they separated."

The term "broken home" is a biased and negatively-loaded concept. Broken homes have been blamed for delinquency, drug addiction, prostitution, and crimes ranging from petty theft to first degree murder. "I don't want you to have anything to do with Johnny," warns a sanctimonious mother. "He's from a broken home." A broken home conjures up images of neglect, confusion, abandonment, rejection, disapproval, and innumerable other hardships. "Broken homes cause broken hearts," one of my clients informed me. When the choice is between a "broken home" and an "unhappy (but intact) home," many people choose the latter. I question their wisdom.

Unfortunately, many automatically equate "divorce" with a "broken home" and all its supposed defects and miseries. They assert that it is a stigma, a telling sign of personal failure, and an inevitable trauma for the children, maintaining that "an unhappy home" is preferable to "a broken home." Yet, if intelligently orchestrated, divorce need not be a bitter crisis or devastating to children.

In my practice of marriage therapy, I am paid to help couples rectify their unhappiness. Perhaps from sentimentality rather than rational judgement, I am inclined to save marriages wherever feasible — especially where young children are involved, and where I believe that the couple is capable of relating harmoniously. But when all efforts to rectify the situation fail, and chronic unhappiness and extreme dissent prevail, I do not hesitate to recommend a constructive and amicable divorce. This results, not in a "broken home," but in two well-functioning, but separate abodes. The following case underscores this point.

Gloria and Hank had seen a marriage counselor and two psychiatrists during their seven-year marriage. Their two sons were six and five. They described themselves and one another as "fantastic parents" despite their inability to get along together. Gloria ran her own lucrative small business, and Hank, who came from a wealthy family, had a high-paying position as vice-president of a large corporation. "We have every reason in the world to be happy," Hank explained. "We love our children, we live in a magnificent home, we drive expensive cars, take frequent vacations — it all sounds like a dream. Most people would gladly trade places with us. And yet we just don't get along."

Sex was a constant problem. "It was okay during the first couple of years," Hank alleged. Gloria snapped, "It was never okay!" Hank looked hurt and said, "You keep changing your story." Gloria impatiently explained, "I am not changing my story. It was tolerable for the first year or so, but it was never okay." This was typical of their interactions. "What's the main problem with sex?" I asked.

Hank answered. "She's never in the mood." Gloria ignored his remark. "I experience a lot of discomfort," she explained. "Except with Derek!" Hank retorted. "Oh boy! Let's not get into that again."

"Who's Derek?" I asked.

It transpired that Derek had been Gloria's lover for the past two years. Their casual affair had intensified and they were now heavily involved. Her relationship with Derek only came to light *after* finding out Hank was having an affair with Gloria's best friend. Derek told Hank that he wished to marry Gloria, to which Hank replied "Gloria can leave any time she wishes, but she leaves without the children." Hank threatened to get "the best lawyer that money can buy" and to fight Gloria "to hell and back" for custody of the children. "I'll never give up my kids!"

A previous therapist recommended "open marriage" as a way of resolving this impasse. Hank said that he was now violently opposed to extramarital sex and insisted that if Gloria were less stubborn, they could work out their differences and have a good relationship. Privately, Gloria confided in me that she had married Hank on the rebound, and that the only thing she ever found attractive about him was his bank balance. She wanted to marry Derek, but she was not prepared to give up her children. "I've told all this to Hank," she said, "but he simply dismisses it from his mind."

I met with Hank privately and tried to persuade him that he was entitled to a woman's love and attention. "Why continue living with Gloria's indifference and constant rejection?" He kept repeating, "I'm not stopping her; she's free to go whenever she likes. I'll gladly give her a divorce. I've even offered her a large cash settlement." He remained adamant about the children. "They stay with me.... I'm not going to become a weekend father or some sort of Santa Claus to my kids."

Gloria's friends had advised her to battle it out in court. "No judge will award Hank the custody of the children," they said. But Gloria was unwilling to take the chance. "And besides," she added, "I don't want to go dragging my children into court." Derek offered to reason with Hank, but they ended up in a brawl which only exacerbated matters.

I met with Gloria and Hank and drew them a verbal portrait of what I saw happening over the course of the next few years unless they resolved their impasse. The tension and destructive feelings between them would inevitably intensify and spill onto the children. How could we prevent this and guarantee four winners instead of four casualties?

To emphasize the destructive consequences of their current situation, I dubbed it *The Game of the Four Losers*. "First let's stop asking what is best for Hank and for Gloria. Let's *really* consider your children. What is best for them?" I hinted that they were both clinging to their children for selfish, if not spiteful, reasons. I stressed that as two caring, loving parents, mutual and easy access to their offspring was a necessary part of any constructive plan. We then examined joint custody options that could best serve the needs of the children.

We discussed child support, alimony, the division of property, geographical boundaries (How far apart should Gloria and Hank live from each other?) and how best to prepare and inform the children of their decisions. These discussions often grew heated, but I was able to mediate a series of sensible and rational agreements which considered the welfare of the entire family. Hank and Gloria were aware that I was not siding with either one of them. Thus, I could turn to Gloria and say, "Oh come now. You can't expect Hank to agree to that idea!" or I would upbraid Hank, "There you go again, putting your needs before those of your children." Potential hostilities were thus transformed into positive energy directed toward constructive ends.

If Hank and Gloria had consulted separate lawyers, inflammatory and adversary interactions would have been almost inevitable. Divorce counseling vigilantly short-circuits the bitterness, the animosity, and the ill-will that most people consider inevitable. It took more than two months for Hank, Gloria and me to arrive at an agreement that the three of us considered equitable and in everyone's best interests. Lawyers were then consulted to draw up the final papers. Gloria's lawyer said, "I can get you a better deal than this. You're selling yourself short." She told him, "You don't know what you are dealing with. Please don't make waves. Believe me, I know what I'm doing. Just put it through as it stands."

Gloria married Derek as soon as the divorce from Hank was finalized. I was last in touch with them about three years after the divorce. Hank had not remarried but was living with a woman. I expressed pleasant surprise when Gloria mentioned that Hank and his girlfriend would be joining her and Derek in taking the children on a trip to Disney World. "That sounds too good to be true," I said. Gloria quipped, "Oh, but we are the products of modern divorce counseling!"

MYTH 15 REVISITED

This myth, of course, overlaps Myth 11 (Having a child will improve a bad marriage) and in my "Revisit," I mentioned the fact the children raised by parents in a loveless and acrimonious household are probably worse off than those whose parents divorce (especially if they do so intelligently). At the end of Page 1, due to dearth of readily available and judicious instructions on marital skills, I wrote: "Most people don't know how to be married!" Similarly, it can also be said that "Most people do not know how to be good parents!"

Several studies have suggested that divorce inevitably takes a toll on children. One well-known writer, Judith Wallerstein, has followed up 60 divorced families since 1971 and reported that half of the children had become psychologically disturbed and maladjusted adults. This was attributed to the divorce per se. But could it be, not the divorce that unhinged the kids, but what had preceded it? For example, could the tense household that prevailed before the parents split up have contributed to the children's problems? Could abuse from one or both parents prior to the divorce have played a significant role? Are children in tense and feuding households better off than those whose parents get divorced? I doubt it! It seems clear that children of warring spouses — whether or not they remain married — will lack role models for loving and caring marital relationships.

It is also important to note that parents often tend to overlook their children's needs, especially in custody battles. Postdivorce visiting arrangements are too frequently made to suit the parents' schedules and convenience at the expense of what is best for the children. And all too often children are not properly prepared to face and understand the divorce. A child wakes up one morning to find that her father and his belongings have disappeared. How and when divorcing parents break the news to their children makes a world of difference to their subsequent adjustment and self-acceptance.

- The main point here is that divorce does not have to be a bitter crisis or prove devastating to children if the parents orchestrate it rationally, with due care and consideration for the best interests of their children in mind.

MYTH 16

A Husband's Ambition Comes Before a Wife's Career

everal specific incidents led me to include this myth in the basic two dozen. One of my colleagues, an accomplished professional woman, had been invited to participate in an international conference that could have opened new doors of opportunity. Madelynne was exhilarated at the prospect. Nevertheless, she turned down the invitation when she learned that her husband would be out of town (at a rather mundane business meeting) and that their daughters, ages ten and eight, were in a school play, and expected at least one parent to be present.

What would justify this decision? Why did her husband's business activities take precedence over Madelynne's professional ventures? Why didn't he offer to forgo his trip so that she could have attended the conference? Would it have damaged the children if both parents were away, leaving them in the hands of a capable babysitter?

A different case involved a corporate male executive, whose wife was a college professor. Juanita drew an annual salary of $30,000; Jerome's earnings, including various stock options and bonuses, was almost ten times higher. When his company's Board of Directors decided to open a branch some two thousand miles away, and selected Jerome to head it up, they seemed to take for granted that Juanita would surrender her tenured professorship, and move away from relatives and friends. I asked Jerome why he automatically assumed that Juanita would walk away from an academic position she had worked extremely hard to obtain. With a slight sneer he said: "She hardly earns enough, after paying taxes, to keep her gas-guzzling Jaguar running for a year!"

Is this a satisfactory and sufficient reason?

The third case illustrates an all too frequent situation. Julienne, upon the birth of her first child, had dropped out of graduate school before completing a doctorate in psychology. She had three more children, yet managed to conduct enough profitable ventures from her home to put her husband through medical school and a residency in ophthalmology. Two days after their seventeenth wedding anniversary, her husband asked her for a divorce. A year later he was married to a twenty-four-year-old nurse. "I wish I had completed my own education," Julienne lamented. "At least I'd have something to fall back on."

The fourth case was the antithesis of each of the foregoing. Sheryll, who had founded and developed her own company, earned more than twice as much as her husband. Yet when Carl had to go on a business trip, Sheryll reacted in the same way as the wives I have already mentioned — she was the one who stayed at home and took care of the house and the children, regardless of pressing commitments at her place of work.

In the first, third, and fourth cases, if the partners were functioning harmoniously despite their unequal footing, it would be fatuous for outsiders to criticize their arrangement. There are many successful "traditional" marriages where the husband is the sole breadwinner, and the wife, a full-time homemaker, sees to it that her husband is at the center of her attention. Those who would wish to rescue these "exploited" women, raise their consciousness, and "liberate" them, would be making a serious error. It is not wise to project one's own values onto someone else's marriage. Thus, those who cringe at the idea of a husband staying at home and performing "feminine" functions — cooking, cleaning, and caring for the children — fail to recognize that for some couples, this arrangement works very well.

In the cases I have mentioned, however, I have evidence that each deeply resented her husband's chauvinistic attitude toward her career or vocation. These resentments had a negative impact on their marriages. (Jerome, who regarded his wife's professorship with disdain — "She hardly earns enough... to keep her gas-guzzling Jaguar running for a year!" — would have been better advised to realize what academic tenure meant to her. The end result may have been no different; that is, Juanita still might have given up her post at the university and moved 2,000 miles away. However, a genuinely sympathetic statement from Jerome to the effect that this would undoubtedly constitute a huge sacrifice for her, would have augured better for their future together.)

Many in our society are still victims of the widespread view that the pursuit of a profitable and truly productive career is an exclusively male prerogative. There are still those who firmly believe that women should not aspire to any role or function other than that of wife or mother. Everyone's psychological well-being requires that he or she be engaged in rewarding and pleasurable activities. Women do not thrive on a life of passivity and dependence. True, many women succeed in making a full-time and rewarding career out of homemaking, and in most cultures, women, not men, are responsible for early child care. Nonetheless, it is any woman's right to break with universal tradition. Women, like men, need not define self-worth in terms of marital and child-rearing practices (See Myth 13).

Both men and women are capable of nurturing and attending to their partners, being caretakers and helpmates, and maintaining viable professional identities. It is my impression that many women — but not as many men — also are capable of having a family and a career, without neglecting either. And why might this be the case? As some psychologists have shown, our society tends to condition and train boys to be autonomous and individualistic, whereas girls learn how to connect emotionally with others. "Masculinity" is still equated with a quest for power; "femininity" ties in with loving and caring. Thus, "career women" often manage to combine "masculine" autonomy with "feminine" warmth and love.

The main point that I am emphasizing is that it is an error for women to downplay their careers for the sake of their mates — and end up resenting them for it. It is even more serious when husbands fail to recognize the importance of their working wives' careers and automatically assume that their own careers are more significant.

MYTH 16 REVISITED

Daily, in our society, fewer and fewer people believe that women should not aspire to any role outside that of a wife and mother. Similarly, it seems that those women who do elect to place home-making at the center of their activities are less likely to encounter pressures to do otherwise. One can be an ardent feminist and still decide to be a stay-at-home-mom!

Every society has different strata, and there are undoubtedly populations in which male dominance is still the prominent *modus vivendi*. But given that it is several decades since the women's movement first came into being, and given that there has been widespread publicity on sexual discrimination and sexual harassment, consciousness raising and greater awareness has been achieved in many areas and domains. I would wager that sexism is on the wane and that a greater degree of egalitarianism prevails than was true when this book first appeared.

Currently, in my own practice, I have seen very few women with the complaints or plights that brought Madelynne, Juanita, and Julienne, and Sheryll into therapy. Instead, equal numbers of women and men seek therapy because the demands of their executive positions prove extremely stress provoking. I have read conflicting reports about the impact that this is having on family life and child rearing.

- In today's world, many couples need to factor into their relationship the conditions imposed upon them by respective work demands. Issues of this kind are usually best examined during premarital discussions. A clear, mutually agreeable plan for the respective careers will help to avoid unpleasant surprises.

MYTH 17

If Your Spouse Wants To Leave, Hang On and Fight

Early one morning I received a telephone call from the wife of an acquaintance. "I don't know what to do and to whom to turn," Vickie said, her distress coming through clearly. I asked: "What's wrong? What's happened?" Straining not to cry, she answered, "Two days ago, Gerald told me that he is in love with another woman and wants a divorce. Since then, I've been unable to eat, or sleep, or do anything except cry. I'm taking Valium and am walking around in a daze. I don't know what to do." As we talked, Vickie told me that her husband had been involved with another woman for ten months and planned to marry her as soon as he and Vickie were officially divorced.

I offered Vickie some sound advice which I was sure she would not follow: "Have Gerald and his girlfriend move in together," I told her. "Permit them to live with each other full-time for three months. If possible, try to have zero contact with your husband during these ninety days, but see to it that you date other men. When the three months are up, meet Gerald for dinner and inquire if he is still so enamored." I explained that by removing the barriers and allowing the lovers to experience unencumbered togetherness, much of the romance would die a natural death (See Myth 2). The best way to get to know people is to live with them for a few months; it is also the best way to destroy illusions.

As expected, Vickie did not follow my advice. Instead, she put up a titanic struggle: hysterics, impassioned beggings and pleadings, threats of suicide. This only made her less attractive and less desirable in her husband's eyes, especially when compared to his paramour, who was at all times composed, but nevertheless deeply concerned. Next, Vickie launched an attack on Gerald's lover, which (he subsequently mentioned to me) only made his wife appear "doubly pathetic." In the end, Vickie lost the battle. By putting obstacles in her husband's path, she had increased the allure of his great romance, and had diminished her own value.

By contrast, a female associate had handled the identical situation entirely differently. When Elizabeth's husband revealed his undying and eternal devotion to another woman and asked for a divorce, all she said was, "I'm really going to miss you!" This was stated quietly, without rancor, but with obvious feeling. There and then, her husband realized his folly and capitulated. In this case, the begging, pleading, threats and recriminations came from his lady friend when she was informed about his change of heart.

I do know of several instances where a spouse's tenacity and endurance prevented the love-smitten partner from ending the marriage, but I see these people as having won Pyrrhic victories. In one case, when the usual tactics failed to work (the rejecting wife was unmoved by her husband's threats, entreaties and appeals), Harvey went on a hunger strike. After four days Nancy finally succumbed and eventually surrendered. She terminated her extramarital liaison and lived unhappily ever after with a metaphorical gun to her head.

The breakup of a marriage is almost always a serious matter, and it is easy to understand why people are so often reluctant or unwilling to let go. Half a loaf may be better than no bread at all, but is half a slice, or perhaps just a few crumbs, sufficient to sustain emotional life? If one of the partners genuinely wants out of the marriage, but stays in because of pity, fear, or money, or guilt, what sort of union do they end up with?

Denial plays an important role in these matters. For instance, when Olga informed Ralph that she had stopped loving him years ago, but had lacked the courage and the wherewithal to leave him sooner, he attributed this to a temporary "phase that she was going through," and refused to take her remarks seriously. When several weeks went by and Olga remained adamant, Ralph still insisted that "she doesn't really mean it." Olga told me how deeply she detested Ralph, how she abhorred his cruelty to animals, his harsh attitude to the children, his judgmental and condemnatory attitudes, his malicious actions, and a host of other negative attributes. She was finally able to plan an escape from "twelve years in the black hole of Calcutta" due to a comfortable inheritance. I met with Ralph and impressed upon him the fact that Olga's antipathy was not a passing phase. Nevertheless he stated that he refused "on principle" to give her her freedom. (Olga and Ralph lived in a country where it was exceedingly difficult to win a contested divorce.)

Ralph never did explain what led him to force the unwilling Olga to remain married to him. The previous eight years must have been as arid for him as they were for her. There was no affection between them; sex amounted to what Olga termed "a rape scene" several times a year; and in the home, Ralph was left to fend for himself. Olga repeatedly yelled, "I hate you!" "I wish you were dead!" and similar deprecating statements to Ralph. When she told him of the other man in her life, he repeated that he would never let her go, "on principle."

Olga finally did get through to Ralph. She delivered a speech that would have chilled most people's blood to the bone. She greeted him one morning more or less as follows: "Ralph, I had a beautiful dream last night. This dream was so vivid; in it, you died. I was so delighted, so overjoyed, that I burst into song. When I woke up and realized it was only a dream, I burst into tears. I want you dead, Ralph. Your death has come to mean more to me than my own life. So I'm giving you fair warning, Ralph — watch out! If I were you, I'd start looking for powdered glass or arsenic in my food." Ralph laughed it off at first, but within seventy-two hours he announced to Olga that he had decided she wasn't worthy of him. She got her divorce.

"Don't go where you are not wanted, and don't stay where you are not wanted." More than a homely aphorism, this advice is a clear message not to stay in any relationship where one is merely tolerated, or pitied, or suffered. Perhaps some people "hang in" because they believe that love can be rekindled. If so, they are victims of Myth 18.

MYTH 17 REVISITED

The main theme here is the inadvisability of staying where one is not wanted. Who wants to be in a relationship based on pity? The way this myth is presented, however, makes it seem that my advice to one and all is simply to throw in the towel if one's spouse asks for a divorce. This was not my intent. For many, the genuine threat of a divorce serves as a wakeup call. Just last week, after having met with a couple for 5 sessions, we reached a happy resolution. The husband had asked his attorney to serve divorce papers on his wife. He had spoken about doing so for quite some time, but upon seeing that he was no longer making idle threats, his wife had pleaded with him to go with her to a marriage counselor. They ended up seeing me, and it soon became clear that some minor changes in the way they treated and responded to each other would make a major difference.

- If your partner is determined to leave you, there's no point in degrading yourself by begging and imploring him or her to stay. But if the situation is not beyond the point of no return and you firmly believe that the relationship is viable, it makes sense to go all out to save it.

Dead Love Can Sometimes Be Rekindled

*I*have met many people who remained in marriages that were emotionally barren and spiritually dead, where love, affection, and caring had long since dried up. Those who finally terminated these oppressive unions often described the experience as "Coming out of a damp, dark hole into the soul-warming sunshine"; or "Being able to see again after being totally blind."

What had kept these desolate, futile marriages alive?

Many dreadful relationships survive because the partners cling to each other out of neurotic fear. Others are held together by concern about public opinion, religious scruples, financial pressures, or similar constraints. Some people become disillusioned upon discovering that marriage offers infinitely less than they had hoped for, yet they muddle through their domestic problems rather than end the relationship.

If there is at least a modicum of companionship in the marriage, some vestige of conjugal affection or sympathetic understanding, it is understandable that people might shun separation and divorce. Most adults recognize companionship, affection, and understanding as the ingredients that maintain the viability of marriage. Yet there persist those unhappy arrangements in which husband and wife despise each other and find virtually everything about the other person irritating, if not infuriating.

In Myth 17, I described situations wherein one partner wished to leave, but the other wanted to preserve the marriage. Here, I am referring largely to those "gruesome twosomes" who both agree that "love is dead," but who vigilantly avoid doing anything about it.

Gordon and Mary had been married for nineteen years; both described the last seventeen as "dreadful." They ran into problems within the first six months but thought nothing of it. "After all," Gordon correctly observed, "there is no family that has absolutely no problems."

Indeed, if only those couples who had zero problems remained married, the divorce rate would be one hundred percent! In *successful* marriages, however, husbands and wives have either learned how to adjust to their problems, or have developed methods of solving them as they arise.

As I listened to Mary and Gordon's account of their marriage, it was obvious that, far from adjusting to or solving their problems, they each had developed defenses that escalated every minor difficulty into a major crisis. Finally, after years of profound unhappiness, this childless couple decided to get a divorce. I was consulted to mediate their divorce settlement prior to their consulting separate attorneys.

From a financial and property settlement standpoint, this divorce posed no undue problems and was exceedingly straight-forward. After two meetings, they had agreed on all the major terms vis-a-vis the house, cars, and bank accounts, and were much relieved to be putting an end to "this travesty of a marriage." The following dialogue ensued:

AAL: What took you so long?

Mary: Stupidity!

Gordon: Yeah, that and inertia.

Mary: I must own up to something else — sentimentality. I'm not talking for Gordon, strictly for myself. I'm a sentimental moron! I kept thinking that things would get better.

AAL: By themselves? I mean why did you think that matters would improve?

Mary: I'm still speaking for myself. During our courtship things were great, at least that's how I remember them.

Gordon: That's true, they were great back then. I'd say that we continued to get along pretty well for the first year or two after we got married.

Mary: Yes. It was no bed of roses, but it was probably as good as most, and a lot better than some.

AAL: And then what?

Mary: If it is possible to fall out of love, just as it is possible to fall in love, I'd say that's what happened — I fell out of love.

AAL: Was this sudden, or did it develop gradually, perhaps insidiously?

Mary: You may laugh, but it was very sudden. Don't ask me when or where or why, but I do remember arriving at the conclusion that I not only no longer loved Gordon, but that I was no longer in love with him.

Gordon: I can relate to that. As we have told you, it's not as if we beat each other up, or threw things around. We both got into smouldering hates that ate us up. I have ulcers and she has migraine headaches. But I can remember reaching a point where something snapped inside me and I absolutely knew I had stopped loving her.

Mary: Obviously, we thought about getting a divorce, and once or twice, we even made preliminary contacts with lawyers.

AAL: And then?

Gordon: Like I said, inertia.

Mary: It was more than that. My best girlfriend is divorced and she was always telling me about the jerks out there. There's an old saying, "The devil you know is better than the devil you don't know." And besides, I used to think that we could rekindle some of those old feelings. It's hard to give up hope.

AAL: So after many years did you finally give up hope?

Mary: Let me ask you a question. Is it possible to revive a dead marriage?

AAL: Is it possible to revive a dead horse, or a dead bug? Dead is dead! You can't rekindle a dead fire. If the fire is dead, totally out, you have to build a new fire. You can only revive, resuscitate, reignite someone or something that has some life left in it, some spark, some glowing ember.

Gordon: I think you're right.

Mary: Are you saying that you can never get back those old feelings?

AAL: Well, I think you can speak from personal experience. You tried. Did you succeed?

Mary: I see what you mean.

Some people believe that they can "make" someone love them. Love cannot be legislated. Lots of people waste energy and time in futile attempts to "win" someone's love. A cousin of mine went out of her way to win back the love of her husband. She took up golf (which she thought would please him). After hardly cooking more than a boiled egg in ten years, she joined a culinary institute and started serving up lavish meals (and spouted cliches about getting to a man's heart via his stomach). She had her hair dyed blonde (because she thought this would appeal to his aesthetic taste). And she expressed enthusiasm for deep sea fishing (something she had eschewed all their married life). Did this help her win back his love? On the contrary. He viewed all of these changes with distrust and said that she had become "pathetic."

When love dies, it remains dead. Trying to bring back that which is dead is like giving mouth-to-mouth resuscitation to a cadaver.

MYTH 18 REVISITED

When a therapist is consulted by a couple who thoroughly dislike (if not despise) each other, is it professionally appropriate to declare the marriage bankrupt, or is this, as some declare, playing God? In these cases I always state my candid opinion – but stress that it is merely an *opinion* and recommend that they consult someone else to see what he or she might conclude. Recently I saw a couple who, in my estimation, are so thoroughly incompatible that it amazes me that they ever got together. She has become truly contemptuous of him; he is extremely critical and scornful of her. Quite frankly, I found it very unpleasant being in the same room with them. I referred them to a colleague who, to my surprise, saw them three times a week, for a very high fee, for many months before concluding, in his words, that they "were a hopeless case." Physicians usually know when to throw in the towel, but many psychologists and counselors try to resuscitate proverbial corpses!

- Too many couples who would be infinitely better off apart from one another stay together in an atmosphere of indifference or even hatred. Some are chained together by their religion. Most remain together out of fear. A loveless marriage is a terrible waste of two lives.

Competition Between Spouses Adds Sparkle to a Marriage

ompetition between husband and wife makes about as much sense as tossing bricks through one's living room window. Competition is corrosive; it insidiously gnaws away at the very fabric of togetherness and trust that forms the basis of any good marriage. A competitive attitude tends to diminish the mutuality, joint striving, and common goals that characterize the interactions of successful couples.

Good marriages rely on cooperative, collaborative, and unified levels of functioning. In highly competitive relationships, the partners are vying for leadership, functioning like rivals instead of teammates. When marriage becomes a contest, a one-on-one tournament, it is common to find strife and conflict, if not cutthroat tactics. It is absurd for husband and wife to expend energy against one another instead of pooling their resources and responding to outside challenges as a twosome.

Competition is highly touted in our society. Without red-blooded American competitiveness, where would our great country be today? "Be number one! Get to the top! Be the best! Winning isn't everything, it's the only thing!" As some psychologists have pointed out, we actually get mixed messages. On the one hand we are exhorted to win, to get ahead, to compete; yet we are also told to be good sports, to cooperate and be effective team members. Hence confusion: To compete, or to cooperate?

It is lamentable that many people decide to enter into the competitive arena against their spouses, to react to them as rivals or enemies. After years of combative, contentious living, these jousting couples ask: "Where did we go wrong?"

Perhaps I should clarify the type of competition which tends to undermine marital stability. When I play tennis against my wife, do I play hard, do I try to score points, do I endeavor to win? Yes I do! Is this not a reflection of the unhealthy competitiveness to which I was alluding? No. I play hard and attempt to score points for the sole purpose of having a good game, of having fun, of enjoying the personal mastery, of having the ball go where I want it to go. I do not enjoy being blown off the court by a superior player; nor do I enjoy playing someone far weaker. A mismatch takes away the fun for both of us. It's more enjoyable to be evenly matched and give each other a good game. This is not the hazardous competition that has mordant consequences.

Yet the tennis court and the bridge table often provide fuel for ferocious flames when husband and wife play on the same side of the net, or at opposite sides of the table. An unforced error, or an incorrect bid, can arouse such ire in the partner that only a rhinoceros in the agonies of protracted labor could bellow any louder. You would imagine that someone's very life was at stake. We have all seen couples emerge from these recreational pursuits with fire in their eyes and hate in their hearts. This kind of competitiveness is most unfortunate, yet not nearly as bad as "ego contests."

Extensive damage accrues when people put their egos on the line, when self-worth, self-esteem, and perhaps one's entire self-concept are brought into play in a contest of wills. Thus my label of "ego contest." Couples who get into an ego battle will show hostile competitiveness not only when engaging with or against each other in games, but also during ordinary conversations with friends (when they try to outshine each other), when dealing with their children (from whom they each attempt to extract more love and credibility), and in all situations involving money, security, and status.

Couples involved in ego-contests are constantly trying to persuade themselves and their partners that they are equal or superior. Such couples disagree about virtually everything — how to elect a president, invest money, raise children, wash windows. Their interactions are like a constant fencing competition; they dare not drop their guards. Every situation poses a threat and calls for bargaining and jostling to gain the upper hand.

This constant struggle requires each party to perpetually insist on his or her rights. Fighting is continual; they keep on competing and they keep on losing. They seem unable to trust anything that comes from the other; even signs of affection are viewed askance. "Who does he think he's kidding?" "She only wants to 'take me for a ride!'"

At a recent dinner party, I observed a couple — both professionals — jockeying for leadership throughout the evening. When he spoke, she corrected him; when she spoke, he contradicted her. At one point, the husband began telling a joke, whereupon the wife angrily shouted, "Stop! That's my joke." He complied and she completed the joke. Later, while she was telling us about a weekend they had spent in Vermont, he insisted that she cease and desist because the Vermont story "belonged" to him. When she refused, the atmosphere grew tense. The two of them would undoubtedly have ended up making public spectacles of themselves were it not for our quick-witted hostess, who ushered the wife out of the room on the pretext of having something private to discuss with her.

Competitive couples often resort to intimidating or threatening behaviors; sometimes they become vicious. These dangerous and unhealthy ego contests go against the grain. If a husband and wife are not a collaborative pair, the main purpose of being married is violated. A marriage worth preserving must reveal evidence of sharing, of coalition, and of the capacity to seek team solutions when disagreements arise. Only a noncompetitive relationship allows one to build up sufficient trust and confidence to be genuine *collaborators* rather than mere *cooperators*.

Like it or not, competition remains a key element in our culture. Nevertheless, it can be confined to the tennis court, the bridge table, and other recreational environments. It is not a healthy basis for a marriage!

MYTH 19 REVISITED

This is one of the important myths. I can but reemphasize that if husband and wife are not close collaborators in life, the main purpose of being married is abandoned.

- By all means compete on the job, on the athletic field, in the stadium, at the card table, or across the tennis net. But in marriage, if you and your partner are not a genuine twosome, if you are competitors instead of being one another's helpmates, teammates, supporters and allies, your marriage is in deep trouble.

MYTH 20

You Should Make Your Spouse Over into "a Better Person"

airly often, people enter marriage with a "Pygmalion complex." Like Henry Higgins of G.B. Shaw's famous play (and Lerner and Loewe's better-known musical adaptation, "My Fair Lady"), many a spouse undertakes to educate and remodel the other. "After Mel and I are married," confides a young fiancee to her friend, "I will make him over into a new man." Perhaps Mel is quite content with his "old self" and has no wish to be remodeled. Even worse, Mel himself many have intentions of transforming his bride into a "new and better" woman!

George Hart came from a good family, a well-to-do family, but one that was not as prominent as his fiancee's. When the pending nuptials between George and Selma Ritter were announced, several people told Mr. and Mrs. Hart that their son was a lucky man. Mr. and Mrs. Ritter were less than ecstatic, but knew better than to oppose their daughter's strong will. Nevertheless, they did tactfully comment that young George was "an uncut diamond." They stated that he required "considerable polishing" before he could really become George Ritter-Hart. Selma agreed fully, and reassuringly told her parents that George was an apt pupil.

Prior to the wedding (under Selma's facile direction), George's entire wardrobe changed, he sported a new hairstyle, shaved off his mustache, and began to drive a different car. He became, in Selma's words "much more elegant." While dancing with her new son-in-law at the wedding ceremony, Mrs. Ritter expressed disapproval concerning his friends. She was especially irritated at the fact that George's best man was of a different religious persuasion. She said, in effect, "In this family you either shape up or ship out!"

While Selma had appointed herself George's counselor, educator, and advisor on their second date (he had ordered the "wrong" wine at a restaurant and had mispronounced some French words on the menu), the remaking of George really started in earnest after the marriage.

First, his "gauche friends" had to be phased out; second, Sunday morning touch football, or volleyball, or baseball (which he looked forward to each week) had to be given up for certain "household responsibilities" (See Myth 10). "You are a married man now," Selma would remind him, "You have a wife to whom you are answerable." Watching football, boxing, or similar sporting events on television were not befitting his new status. His taste in music had to be upgraded — in fact, George's entire level of aesthetic appreciation called for refinement. Sex was always on Selma's terms and remained within the strict confines of propriety — pretty much "lights off and hands off."

By the time I met George, four months after the wedding, he was unhappy and confused (to say the least). When I completed his life history inquiry, it seemed to me that for George, life with Selma held about as much joy as incarceration in a Turkish prison. "What attracted you to Selma?" I asked. "The Ritters, as you probably know," he said to me, "are a hotshot family. I foolishly went for the glamour, the symbols, the external trappings of success." I asked if Selma would meet with me so that we could try to determine whether or not to salvage the marriage. Selma refused. "Ritters don't believe in that sort of thing!" The marriage was annulled.

It took George only a few months to reach the conclusion that he had entered into an untenable *guerre à outrance* (war to the uttermost). However, I have seen dozens of couples locked in mortal combat, one sculpting the other in his or her own image, both living lives of mutual frustration and vexation, for *years.*

The arrogance of those people who insist that their view of the world is the one and only "right way" is exceeded only by those who are also determined to inflict this view on others!

The idea that it is a husband's or wife's right to educate and make over the other person goes hand-in-hand with the notion that "things will get better after we are married." Things that are bad before marriage tend to get *worse* afterwards. A person who is short-tempered, selfish, sexually unresponsive, and personally intrusive but who promises that things will get better after we are married, should be viewed with extreme skepticism and suspicion by any would-be marriage partner.

Many people have *rescue fantasies.* I call this the "Dick Diver syndrome" (from F. Scott Fitzgerald's *Tender Is The Night,* in which psychiatrist Dick Diver falls in love with his patient Nicole, marries her, and then becomes a mental and physical wreck himself). Medical doctors are especially prone to this fantasy. I have seen several physicians married to people for whom they were doctors first and foremost. Indeed, many physicians know how to relate only to sick people; as long as the person is horizontal, the doctor can display a bedside manner that exudes charm and caring. When the person recovers, the doctor withdraws.

Marriages based on the rescue fantasies of one or both partners are invariably exceedingly complex, but the end results are often predictable. To satisfy the rescuer's desire for power, approval, or control, the recipient must continue to be (or appear to be) needy. These relationships seldom stand the strain of readjustment to an equal footing. Frequently, the rescuer turns out to be far more emotionally indigent than the person being rescued. Rescuers invariably feel that they are entitled to eternal gratitude; those who have been rescued resent having to be forever-more beholden.

"We married for the wrong reasons" is a frequent expression of couples where one or the other was intent upon changing — rescuing — his or her partner.

The moral of the story? Get married on the grounds of compatibility and caring, where common interests, attitudes, and feelings may call for slight adjustment but no major changes. And leave rescuing to lifeguards, firefighters, and emergency medical teams.

MYTH 20 REVISITED

There's not much that I can add to or subtract from this account of a common error. While the unmitigated arrogance of a Selma Ritter is rather appalling, a good marriage does tend to enhance positive attributes while correcting negative aspects. For example, when one of my friends (whom we had all viewed as a committed bachelor) got married, we noticed several changes for the better. Apart from seeming much happier, he was better groomed (he no longer wore stained, torn and ill-fitting clothes, and his ear and nose hairs had been trimmed), and he claimed to be extremely pleased to be living in an attractive townhouse in place of his cluttered one-room apartment.

- Modest makeovers are par for the course. True compatibility may call for minor adjustments but no major changes.

MYTH 21

Opposites Attract and Complement Each Other

*I*t is not uncommon for an outgoing, vivacious, and extraverted person to attract someone who is more intellectualized, controlled, and introverted. Insecure folks may seek "strong silent types" who can offer stability and security. Steady, highly controlled persons tend to view more spontaneous potential mates as warm, vital, fun-loving creatures, who can offset the serious side of life.

Such opposites are sometimes drawn to each other's different styles of living. As friends and lovers, for a short time, they usually relate well, and do in fact find a complementary relationship which tends to neutralize some of their own inadequacies and liabilities. But if they marry, their different outward styles clash, and bring them face-to-face with the fundamental differences between them. Her flamboyance and flirtatiousness become sore points; his staid and predictable behaviors create ennui. He withdraws and she feels rejected; she frantically attempts to regain her ground, but he feels criticized and withdraws further. Soon a power struggle takes over, and both resort to tactics that undermine the true intimacy they each desire.

That unfortunate sequence is drawn from reports in the psychological literature and from my own clinical observations.

Polar opposites may find one another enjoyably different and alluring for a limited time. Long-term relationships usually flourish when similarity rather than dissimilarity prevails.

The popular film and television series, "The Odd Couple", capitalized on the clashes that arose when a slob lived with an immaculate perfectionist. In a marriage where one partner is extremely fussy and fastidious, clashes are likely if the other is disorganized and sloppy. The myth suggests that, if the perfectionistic partner enjoys cleaning up after the messy one, harmony will reign — especially if the slob appreciates someone who straightens things up.

Incessant nagging to clean up, stop messing, and be more considerate typically interferes with more important issues and results in mutual antagonism. I have treated innumerable couples in which an obsessive-compulsive housewife drove her husband to drink, or a houseproud obsessional husband demanded such perfectionism that his wife had a "nervous breakdown."

As I have underscored throughout this book, good marriages call for similarities, not dissimilarities. I know an excellent marriage in which both partners were extraordinarily compulsive. In tight-fitting unison, they worked shoulder to shoulder, shining the brass doorknobs in their home, polishing the parquet floors, scrubbing the walls, and doing minor repairs. (I always thought of their house as a museum, but they seemed happy with it.) While other people were enjoying picnics, boating, going to the beach, playing tennis, this couple preferred to be doing something around the house. Had either married a less compulsive person, friction would have been inevitable. (Compulsive people are usually rigid by nature and have difficulty making concessions.)

When people with opposing views and dissimilar tastes spend much time together, certain clash-points are inevitable.

- Picture a couple wherein one member is fond of talking, of sharing feelings and ideas, while the other is a very private person who enjoys solitude and wants to be alone.

- Or think of a gregarious person who loves being with other people and seeks out the company of many different types of individuals, married to a loner who basically distrusts and dislikes the vast majority of other people.

- Or take a fiery, passionate, highly-sexed individual married to someone with a low sex drive.
- Consider a miser being attracted to a spendthrift and marrying that person.

How much marital bliss would be likely to ensue in each of the instances mentioned?

Happy marriages require that *basic* similarities outweigh dissimilarities. Tremendous clashes arise over different philosophies of *child-rearing*, and many a divorce has resulted from differences of opinion in this regard. If people have very different tastes in matters pertaining to *leisure and fun* (sports, vacations, outings), problems are bound to arise. And where profound differences in *values* are noted (e.g., regarding attitudes, religious beliefs, political leanings), strife is almost a certainty.

The "opposites attract and make good marriage partners" myth probably arose from the fact that *some* differences can be enriching, stimulating, even exciting and fascinating. Only a committed narcissist would desire to marry a clone! But it is a quantum leap from the fact that slight differences can prove beneficial to the notion that polar opposites make good marriage partners.

MYTH 21 REVISITED

Recently, some national magazines published articles about well-known couples who seemed to thrive despite basic differences. Some of these happily married couples had opposite views about politics; others were in opposite camps vis-à-vis religious beliefs. The media were, in fact, wrongly claiming that opposites not only attract one another but also enjoy better marriages than like-minded individuals. There are probably exceptions to virtually all rules, but certain differences spell marital doom. Similarity, likeness, congruence, and sameness tend to create successful happy marriages.

- Slight differences can enhance a relationship, but significant differences will tend to destroy it.

MYTH 22

Couples Should Not Reveal Personal Matters to Outsiders

*I*t was several years ago that I first realized the full implications of this myth. A good friend was confiding in me about his marriage. He revealed that although he loved his wife, he found her hard to get along with. He referred to her moodiness, and to the fact that she was often unappreciative; he added that she tended to be a grievance collector, and that she was sexually inhibited.

Hearing all of this, I suggested that perhaps marriage therapy might be advisable. "I'm afraid that's out of the question," he said. After a few seconds he elaborated. "Rose is dead set against all forms of counseling and therapy. She feels that people should not discuss any personal matters with outsiders." He then went on to say that if Rose ever found out that he had told me intimate details about their relationship, "All hell would break loose — it would be worse than World War III." I have since discovered that this attitude is anything but rare.

Over the years, individuals deeply distressed about their marriages have consulted me only after making absolutely certain that their spouses would never find out that they had spoken to a therapist. They referred to several common themes: What is between husband and wife should not leak outside the marriage. What is between husband and wife is no one else's business. Revealing marital secrets to anyone is a gross betrayal.

People who subscribed to any of the foregoing notions often felt deeply guilty after confiding in me. "Perhaps Sammy is right," a distressed wife said after discussing her marriage problems, "Perhaps I shouldn't have told a perfect stranger about what goes on in our home." A husband said: "It probably is wrong to discuss your marital problems with anyone other than your mate, but lately I have been feeling desperate." Yet another opinion went even further: "We are Roman Catholics but my wife feels that we should never speak to anyone, including a priest, about *us*."

These secretive people are reflecting beliefs that are widespread in our culture. There is a tendency to be over-zealous about privacy. The script is: "Keep all your opinions to yourself; reveal as little as possible to others." A young man informed me that his father's oft-repeated motto was, "Even a fish would not get into trouble if it kept its mouth shut!"

While I am not advocating that people wear their hearts on their sleeves, or that they indiscriminately open up to just anyone, there is psychological evidence that *selective* self-disclosure is necessary for emotional health. Good friendships, for instance, are predicated upon a high degree of sharing and deliberate transparency (see Myth 1). Yet people often elect to remain opaque — they erroneously believe that it is to their advantage to be seen as mysterious and enigmatic.

One underlying reason for keeping others at a distance is the fear that to be totally known for oneself automatically guarantees dislike, if not contempt and disparagement, from others. Moreover, many people believe that if outsiders (and that means any and all other people) gain access to intimate and personal facts, they will use such information destructively. Thus, people put up phony fronts and hide behind facades. Their hearts could be breaking, but no one would guess it from their glistening veneers. Their authentic selves remain hidden behind several masks.

For many years, I have been struck by a disquieting phenomenon. Anyone who has watched news coverage on TV has undoubtedly seen shocking stories aired from time to time about seemingly peace loving citizens who, without warning, went berserk and butchered their families with a hatchet or a shotgun. Typically, neighbors are interviewed and are invited to comment on the perpetrators and their families. I have been impressed by the number of times these unfortunate people were described as "very private," as "keeping to themselves," as being outwardly friendly but basically unknown to their neighbors. It is the belief of many psychologists that if such people had frankly disclosed their genuine thoughts and feelings to some friend or neighbor, their tragic endings could probably have been averted.

As I think back over the years of my own marriage, when differences arose between my wife and me, we often discussed our hurts or annoyances with mutual friends. Most of them reciprocated. We might have been out for dinner with another couple, or in the company of a few couples, and asked for permission to bounce around some feelings or opinions. Each presented matters from a personal point of view and usually a lively discussion ensued. Although these friends were not psychologists, psychiatrists, or trained marriage counselors, I found it enormously helpful to get their input, to see things from another's point of view. Significantly, there were two couples who never revealed their own hangups, who were willing to listen to us and to the others who self-disclosed, but who kept their own interactions strictly private. I think there is some causal connection between their closemouthed, self-contained posture and the fact that both couples ended up divorced.

In my psychological practice, I have found couples' groups of inestimable value. When four to six couples meet with me regularly for many weeks, I invariably find that the participants gain helpful hints, useful ideas, better ways of communicating and negotiating, perhaps even more from one another than from my professional input. This process has turned around many a marriage that might otherwise have ended in a needless divorce or, perhaps even worse, would have continued lamely staggering along. By opening up to outsiders (especially to well-trained professional outsiders) distressed couples make it possible to find constructive solutions to their problems. (See also Myth 24.)

MYTH 22 REVISITED

The main point here is that very private people live in emotional prisons because they tend to become disconnected from others and from themselves. Growth and intimacy are developed by sharing one's feelings with trusted others. This is not to say that there's any virtue in becoming one of those blabbermouths who tell you the most personal details of their lives within the first five minutes of meeting them. Selective self-disclosure is what is being advocated.

• Being too private is just as detrimental as being too public.

Don't Have Sex When You're Angry

I have left one of the best (worst?) myths for second to last. In any dysfunctional marriages, sex is used as a weapon, a battering ram; it serves as a wedge that drives the couple further and further apart. I have treated many people who foolishly used sex to manipulate their partners. I have lost count of the number for whom sex was at the core of issues concerning power and control. Perhaps the most prevalent theme was that unless everything was going well, unless there were no bad feelings, no ongoing tensions, sexual intercourse could not take place.

One young couple who consulted me were having just such marital and sexual difficulties. Abby was one of those people I have just described — sex was totally outlawed if she was in any way, shape, or form annoyed with her husband. If Robert wished to go to bed with her, he had to be on his best behavior. I asked a blunt question: "What would he need to do in order to get laid tonight?" Abby answered in a very matter-of-fact tone: "Well, I need some help with the house. He could start by vacuuming the living room and den; I've been asking him for months to fix our back fence; and then there's his closet that needs tidying up and sorting out." She would have continued, but I interrupted her by pointing out that if he performed all of those chores, he'd be too tired for sex.

With another couple, the husband was the criterion setter. "Before I can even consider having sex, things have to be right between Paula and me. I have to feel really good about her and vice versa. I need to feel that we have been close and loving, that we are a team. I need to experience her warmth and caring, her fondness and closeness." And how often were all of these criteria met? "Approximately once a month — or less," Paula said plaintively.

In the two cases I have just mentioned, several myths seem to be intertwined with the main one we are addressing. One of them is that love is a necessary component of gratifying sex. In our culture, love and sex have been so inextricably linked that "making love" is a synonym for sexual intercourse. Love is not a commodity that can be manufactured! (The ridiculousness of this euphemism came to the fore when a friend and I drove past two dogs copulating on the street, and she inquired if I had noticed the animals "making love!") Those who view love as an essential precursor for sex tend not to be aware that love often grows out of sex. When people like each other, are attracted to each other, and have good sex with each other, love is likely to develop in time.

Another myth that relates to the one I am emphasizing is that *Sexual relations between husband and wife should always be a special, deeply erotic and yet affectionate and highly satisfying union.* This would be tantamount to insisting that every meal should be an Epicurean delight, served only on the best china and crystal, with soft music, and subdued lights. To grab a quick sandwich would be unthinkable! The person who will eat only in four-star restaurants and nowhere else might go hungry most of the time and become seriously undernourished. If every sexual encounter has to be a four-star performance, the couple will miss out on those delightful "quickies" and less elaborate coital activities that tend to promote intimacy, caring, and physical relief. Those who want nothing but perfect sex usually end up feeling frustrated and starved.

Some couples wait for anger to subside, or spend hours trying to diminish emotional hassles by talking about their feelings (thereby often only increasing their levels of distress).

There are many couples, however, who find that sex diminishes anger. When they are upset or annoyed with each other they go to bed and "work it out" sexually. These partners never allow the pressures to stand in the way of gratifying sex and often find that things fall into perspective — post-orgasmically. I am not suggesting that there is no room for the discussion of feelings in a marriage. Obviously, couples do best when they communicate freely and when they share and air their grievances. I am objecting to those diatribes that so often go on tediously hour after hour, frequently adding up to no more than filibusters designed to avoid sexual intimacy.

Some people subscribe to the *Don't go to sleep angry* myth. In an attempt to "make up," they often end up fighting into the early hours of the morning. I say that after a good night's rest, it is amazing how rapidly one can clear up misunderstandings. A related myth that seems to underlie most of the issues is that *Love and good sex go together*. In truth, many have found that despite great love and affection of their partners, sex *per se* was less than satisfactory, whereas with someone else — where love was not even present — sex was great. In some cases, love can detract from sex. As one person put it: "When I love someone, I have so many different feelings — warmth, obligation, concern, caring, vulnerability, compassion — that my sexual turn-on becomes diluted. But when I am simply physically infatuated, I can really concentrate on sex."

Love messages and sex messages are not synonymous. Those who are deeply in love may, at times, find themselves concentrating so much on the affectionate component that their sexual impulses become "diffused" and result in decreased erotic stimulation.

Those who absolutely insist that sex and love must go together, and that anger, resentment, or irritation must be cleared out of the way before loving sex can ensue, will find themselves shortchanged. Couples who learn to enjoy a variety of sexual ambiences — loving sex, erotic sex, lustful sex, playful sex, even angry sex — are likely to have fewer conflicts and better marriages than those who limit their range of sexual expression.

MYTH 23 REVISITED

The main theme here is that those who place demands on their spouses – be they sexual or nonsexual – will inevitably create resentment and end up paying a huge price. People who use sex as a weapon make an enormous mistake. Anyone who has an elaborate set of preconditions that must be met before having sex with his or her partner is asking for trouble.

- Demanding people are difficult to live with and inevitably create irritation and displeasure. In the sexual area, too many rules and regulations can only undermine the joy and intimacy of good sex.

MYTH 24

Be Satisfied With What You've Got

Unlike some of the myths we have discussed in which it is obvious that the ideas espoused are not only wrong but are also distinctly counterproductive, this one is tricky. Every marriage calls for accommodation, adjustment, and the ability to overlook various provocations or annoyances. We must come to terms with the fact that our partners are bound to have some irritating habits, mannerisms, and modes of conduct that are unlikely to change. One either learns to live with and accept these minor annoyances, or one becomes an incessant nagger.

There are those whose marriages are very good but, because their heads are filled with impossible romantic expectations (Myth 2), they erroneously perceive their relationships to be on the rocks. In many of these instances, what they have turns out to be far superior to what they may actually end up getting. If we can persuade these perfectionists or romanticists to abandon their idealistic strivings and to be satisfied with what they have, they will be far better off.

On the other hand, I am convinced that there are countless marriages which can be significantly enriched and enhanced, transformed from wearisome unions into something quite vital and enriching. People who believe that nothing can be done to improve matters are usually incorrect. One of the most gratifying aspects of my own professional endeavors is the number of floundering marriages (that probably would have continued to flounder, or may have come apart) that I have helped to become relationships well worth preserving.

A Case in Point

Simon and Cindy had been to two marriage counselors. Their ten years of marriage had been turbulent. Marriage counseling had only made matters worse. "The first counselor we saw was a very sweet person, but all she did as far as I could tell was sit there and cluck sympathetically. The second counselor seemed to encourage us to fight in front of him. He gave us padded bats and had us hit each other. I think this only made us feel even madder at each other."

As Cindy was telling me about these experiences, Simon was nodding his head in agreement. Then he spoke up:

Simon: Yeah, your colleagues are real jerks. So why should I believe you're any different? As far as I'm concerned, you're guilty until proven innocent. Frankly, I think you shrinks are all a bunch of yo-yos.

Cindy: Simon, how can you insult the doctor like that!

AAL: He has every right to be skeptical and challenging. In his shoes I would feel the same way. But I have known Simon for about ten minutes whereas you, Cindy, have known him more than ten years. So let me ask you something. I pick up a lot of anger in him, and I would say that his style stinks. Is that true of him in other situations, or only in here with me?

Cindy: You hit the nail on the head. That's what I've been living with for ten years. He doesn't know how to come across like a human being. Why do you think so many people hate him? Why do you think he has trouble with his boss at work? He acts and feels and thinks like a five-year-old. The trouble with him is that inside he doesn't feel like a man, he sees himself as a kid. And he is a total putdown artist!

Simon: I've heard that one before.

AAL: Excuse me. Cindy, how do you know that Simon feels like a child and thinks like a five-year-old? Has he told you so?

Cindy: It's more than obvious.

AAL: Are you ready for Rule Number One? Here it comes: Never tell another person what he or she is thinking or feeling.

Simon: Are you kidding! She's such a goddam mind reader that if you took that away from her she would be speechless.

AAL: Simon, do you really feel more like a boy than like a man?

Simon: I guess sometimes.

AAL: Like when?

Simon: I dunno. I guess when I feel on the spot, sort of intimidated.

AAL: Do I intimidate you?

Simon: No.

Cindy: He's intimidated by his own shadow!

AAL: Hold it! I see part of the trouble here. Cindy, Simon, both of you are what Cindy called "putdown artists." You are both on the warpath, both attacking on all fronts. A marriage implies that you are in the same boat, but you two are punching holes in the bottom of your boat. If you really want it to sink that's alright with me, but if you truly want this marriage to work, you are both going to have to patch up those holes pronto! This translates first and foremost into being nice to one another, talking respectfully, not mind-reading.

Simon: Wouldn't that be a change!

AAL: Well let's do it, starting right now. Let's continue discussing your feelings and your clash points like three civilized adults.

Of course, Cindy and Simon frequently resorted to their usual combative tactics, but the moment one of them stepped out of line, I immediately asked for a "civilized and mature" restatement. We finished the session on an up note.

It took me over a year to help Cindy and Simon become capable of routinely dealing with each other in adaptive, cooperative, mutually respectful ways (See Myth 9). If Cindy or Simon had really felt that no changes could occur, that they may as well settle for their tense and hostile marriage or get a divorce, they would not have consulted me. Fortunately, they were not willing to "be happy with what they had." Despite two fruitless prior experiences with marriage counselors, they cared enough about their relationship to give it a third try and came up winners.

You may have noticed some differences between my active style with Cindy and Simon and the approaches they described to me from their previous counselors. In the final chapter of this book, I'll give you some tips on selecting an effective marriage therapist. When you are ready for "more than you've got," you'll know how to find the help you need to get it!

MYTH 24 REVISITED

There are undoubtedly many couples in stale, dull, unsatisfying relationships who falsely believe that "this is as good as it gets." If there is sufficient basic compatibility and a clear feeling of mutual fondness, good professional help can usually clear away the debris that may conceal a solid underlying foundation. I am also confident that many couples can significantly improve their relationships, if they pay heed to the salient points in this book that pertain to them and then apply each recommendation. The bad news is that an insufficiency of compatibility, a dearth of positive feelings, and a plethora of disdain call for a parting of the ways — amicably orchestrated one would hope.

- It is possible to enrich a ho-hum, blah and tedious marriage if there is more than a modicum of affection between the partners. Intelligent professional help is often indicated in such instances.

...And What Can Be Done About It

*I*f you have read through the two dozen myths and given thoughtful consideration to the arguments advanced, I believe you will notice benefits in your own marriage (present or future). Whether or not you agree with all of my conclusions, a careful examination of your own relationship in the light of these myths will help you avoid the pitfalls that so many couples experience.

Here are some major points I hope you'll remember:

- In most successful marriages, the partners do not live "in each other's pockets" but allow a good deal of mutual freedom and space.

- Successful partners aim for conjugal affection rather than romantic excitement, and are sufficiently respectful of one another to realize that it takes some effort to keep their mates interested (without succumbing to the notion that this necessarily calls for "hard work").

- Intelligent marriage partners are not complacent; they live with a tinge of insecurity and perceive one another as capable of attracting and being attracted to other people.

- Happy marriages are predicated on a capacity to negotiate, compromise, and avoid rigid roles or categorical imperatives. This calls for a degree of maturity, with both partners accepting responsibility for their own happiness.
- In successful marriages there is no mind-reading (i.e., telling the other person what he or she is thinking or feeling), and there are no attempts at reconstructing one another (i.e., trying to "make your spouse over" into a better person).

One Plus One Equals...

If a marriage is to succeed and keep on succeeding, unity across several dimensions is essential.

Unity of goals. Compatibility requires some similar attitudes, at least on the crucial aspects of life together. The way partners act with each other, their children, other family members, and outsiders, must be mutually acceptable.

Unity of togetherness. The way people budget their time has a strong impact on a marriage. No two people have identical personalities, and it is therefore essential for couples to learn how to subordinate some of their individual desires for the sake of each other. If compromises are not forthcoming, clash points can be guaranteed. If too many concessions are required, the couple tends to drift apart. If excessive time is devoted to the achievement of personal ambitions, marital breakdown is probable.

Unity of outlets. Some agreement is necessary on recreational, educational, religious, and economic activities. Without common interests, tensions build and disorganization ensues. Unless a husband's and wife's individual interests and activities are integrated somewhat, a successful marriage cannot be achieved. Everyone has to utilize many resources in working out a satisfactory marriage relationship. The more similar the couple's interests, the easier it is for them to reach mutually agreeable goals.

How Is YOUR Marriage?

Marital relationships are complex institutions. In order to improve the quality of a marriage, it helps to take a systematic look at how it is functioning. Over the past five years, I have used the following questionnaire as a general guide for working with couples in my practice.

MARITAL SATISFACTION QUESTIONNAIRE

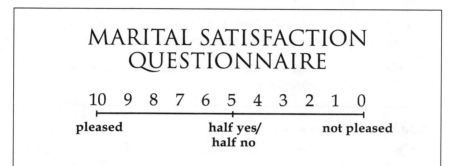

```
10   9   8   7   6   5   4   3   2   1   0
```

pleased   **half yes/**   **not pleased**
                           half no

After each question please write down the number that most closely approximates your present feelings about your marriage or your spouse.

I AM:

(1) Pleased with the amount we talk to each other

(2) Happy with the friends we share in common

(3) Satisfied with our sex life

(4) In agreement with the amount of time you or we spend at work and at home

(5) In agreement with the way we are spending money

(6) Pleased with the kind of parent you are (This refers to the way your spouse interacts with the children.)

(7) Of the opinion that you are "on my team"

(8) Pleased with our leisure time together (e.g., sports, vacations, outings, etc.)

(9) Basically in agreement with your outlook on life (e.g., values, attitudes, religious beliefs, politics, etc.)

(continues on next page)

(10) Generally pleased with the way you relate to members of your own family (This refers to your spouse's parents, siblings, etc.)

(11) Satisfied with the way you relate to members of my family (This refers to your own parents, siblings, ...)

(12) Pleased with your general habits, mannerisms, and overall appearance

---

Add up your total score:

- 84 and more means that you have a VERY GOOD marriage.
- Between 72–83 reflects SATISFACTORY to GOOD feelings and interactions.
- A score of 61–71 suggests that you need to make some basic changes.
- Below 60 indicates a POOR level of marital satisfaction.

When making use of this questionnaire in my practice, I pay attention to both the overall score and the individual scores. Each partner may have scored the marriage in excess of 84 points but may reflect one or two items in the 3, 2, 1, or even zero range. Clearly, any item that is in the "not pleased" zone calls for specific attention.

Marriages that are bankrupt usually call for divorce counseling so that the husband and wife part amicably. (Recently, I saw a couple who obtained a total of 14 combined points — the wife scored 6 points and the husband scored 8. Usually, people whose levels of satisfaction are that low don't consult psychologists — they head straight for the lawyers!)

Nevertheless, many marriages can be improved so that couples can experience more joy than grief. People who believe that nothing can be done to improve a bad marriage are usually incorrect. It is difficult, but not impossible, to transform a poor marriage into a good one.

In the following sections, I've described three procedures which my clients have found valuable aids for relationship improvements.

The Triple-Increase Technique

Here is a technique that many marriage trainers have found extremely effective, and one that you and your partner can readily use without aid of a professional. The husband is asked to make a list of three specific behaviors that he would like his wife to *increase*; the wife is asked to compile a list of the three things she would like her husband to *increase*.

(The requests are expressed in terms of increases rather than decreases so that they come across more positively. The difference is evident in comparing the following two questions:

"Why don't you stop biting your nails so that your hands wouldn't look so ugly?"

"Why don't you increase the length of your nails so that your hands will look more attractive?"

Clearly, the first question sounds over-critical; the second has a positive ring to it.)

When compiling the list of three behaviors, couples often start out far too vague and general. Statements such as "I would like him to increase his level of communication," or "I would like her to increase her concern and caring," are too nebulous. They need to be expressed in terms of *specific* behaviors. For example: "After dinner, I would like to increase the time from five minutes to fifteen minutes for us to sit and chat." "When I get home from the office I would like you to increase the number of times I am greeted with a hug and a kiss." Here are the lists drawn up by one of my couples in treatment.

I want Maurice to increase:

1) The amount of time he spends helping the children with their homework.

2) The number of days he gets back home from work before 6:30 p.m.

3) The number of times he is willing to cuddle without having to have sex.

I want Clara to increase:

1) The number of times she cooks a hot meal for dinner.

2) The occasions that she invites my parents to our house.

3) The amount of time she keeps me company in my basement workshop instead of watching TV.

After each partner has compiled the list the next step is to inquire if the specific items are acceptable to the other partner. If not, they have to be modified. When the couple agrees that the specific requests are reasonable, the focus then shifts to the implementation of each item. In the foregoing case, Martin would be asked to specify exactly how much time he is willing to devote to helping the children with their homework. He then is asked to write down his pledge: "I agree to spend 30-40 minutes, three nights a week, helping the kids with their homework." "I will be home before 6:30 p.m. at least twice a week."

Sometimes, couples prefer to make trade-offs. "If you get home from work before 6:30 p.m. at least three nights next week, I agree to invite your parents 'round over the weekend."

The main point about the triple-increase technique is that it provides six important behaviors that get written into the marital script. This generally results in increased levels of satisfaction.

This procedure can be undertaken as a self-help exercise by couples who are genuinely committed to working cooperatively on the relationship. It is certainly worth a try.

"The Doctor Prescribes..."

Here is another simple tactic that has proved effective with many of the couples I have seen in marital therapy. I call this *prescribed dinners.* Typically, I tell my clients to set aside one evening a week in which they go out for dinner — just the two of them. It need not be anything lavish — a simple diner or hamburger house will do.

The point is that they are to view this night out as a regular appointment, a definite commitment. They would have to have an extremely valid reason to cancel or postpone any prescribed dinners. I tell them: "Over dinner, I want you to imagine that you are out on a date, or that you are in the midst of courtship. Thus, you will try to be as pleasant and as stimulating as possible. This is not the place for quarreling or for discussing problems. It is time for mutual enjoyment and support." This tactic is especially good for busy professional couples whose marital discord stems primarily from the fact that they are both too busy to spend sufficient time together.

Time-limited Intercommunication

Here is a powerful technique that has worked wonders with many of my clients who were willing to use it regularly. It is especially valuable in those situations where one or both parties feels misunderstood. Many couples have complained to me that they feel improperly heard by one another. "Brian doesn't hear half the things I tell him!" "Zelda doesn't really listen when I talk!" This fundamental lack of communication is frustrating in and of itself, but even worse, it often breeds additional resentment and mis-understanding.

Here is what I recommend in these instances:

Set aside at least three, separate, half-hour-long appointments with each other every week for the next month. These sessions are to be taken very seriously and must be viewed as high priorities. Ideally, to derive the greatest benefit from this exercise you need five things — a quiet room where you will not be interrupted; an automatic timer; pencil; paper, and a coin.

Flip the coin to determine who talks first. Set the timer for five minutes. During these five minutes the talker discusses whatsoever he or she pleases. *The listener may not interrupt.* He or she may take notes in preparation for clarification or rebuttal, but no verbal output is to occur until the five minutes elapse and the bell rings (unless the other person does not require the full five-minutes and says "I'm through for now.").

When the timer goes off, the talker is to stop immediately whatever he or she is saying. At that point, the listener paraphrases (repeats back the essence of) the speaker's message. If the speaker is not satisfied with the listener's feedback, he or she says, "You haven't got it quite right," and proceeds to explain to the listener where he/she went wrong. The listener paraphrases again and again until the speaker is fully satisfied. Once the speaker feels that he/she has been properly listened to and understood, he/she says "That's right," or "Thank you, you heard me." The timer is then set for another five minutes, with the previous listener now doing the talking under the same ground rules.

In a typical half-hour session, each person usually has two separate five-minute opportunities to speak. If the paraphrases are brief and accurate, couples may take a few extra minutes and each have three talking and listening periods. At the end of the session, it is important to hug each other and to drop any further discussion of the issues that were raised until the next preset appointment.

Some couples prefer to spend an hour in time-limited inter-communication. I do not recommend more than sixty minutes even for those who favor "mental marathons." One purpose of having these dialogues *time-limited* is to avoid the lengthy nit-picking debates in which certain couples indulge. On the other hand, I have noted that many people tend to require less time to speak and be heard after adhering to the basic rules for several weeks. After a while, only one party may feel the need to speak and be heard on a given occasion, and a three-minute "speech" followed by a 30-second paraphrase may suffice to keep open the channels of communication.

As self-help resources, the three techniques presented in this chapter *(triple increase, prescribed dinners,* and *time-limited inter-communication)* can be very effective if carefully used.

Marriage Counseling, Marriage Therapy, Marriage Training — Who Really Helps?

I have often heard highly skeptical, if not downright pessimistic views expressed about the chances of improving a bad marriage, of converting an unhappy household into one that functions har-moniously and yields emotional rewards worth perpetuating. Why do many people scoff at the idea that professional interventions can have beneficial effects? That dysfunctional marriages can become gratifying and relatively untroubled partnerships?

One reason is that few people realize that there is a difference between *marriage counseling* and *marriage therapy/marriage training*. Many marriage counselors adhere to a "nondirective" philosophy, in which they merely reflect the clients' emotional turmoils — holding up a "psychic mirror" as it were, so the couple can see themselves in a clearer perspective. These counselors never give advice; they believe in bringing hidden agendas to the fore so that people can then "work things out for themselves." Many clients find this nondirective approach extremely frustrating. They want answers, guidance, active assistance — and in my view, they are entitled to no less.

Another reason many people are uncertain about marriage counseling is that many therapists consider it necessary to examine their clients' childhoods, spending a great deal of time discussing the past. Mental health practitioners have myths too, and some of them interfere with professional effectiveness. Many of my colleagues incorrectly believe that people need to discover *why* they are the way they are, *why* they do things they do, *why* they feel the way they feel. Actually, people would be infinitely better off if more professionals realized that the what is more powerful than the *why* when it comes to changing behavior. The question to ask is: *What can be done* to change matters most rapidly and long lastingly? *Why* may satisfy one's curiosity, but does little to bring about improvement.

Marriage Training rests on several assumptions:

- Psychological change calls for problem *solving here and now*, rather than preoccupation with *there and then*.

- Marital problems arise from *misinformation* (for example, believing the myths described in this book) and from *missing information* (that is, not having the skills or ability to cope with certain demands).

- *Talking* about marriage problems is necessary but insufficient — the therapist must devise active means of *solving* these problems.

- Both partners must be willing to work at the marriage and make an effort to change.

As may be inferred from the foregoing suppositions, a marriage therapist or trainer, as I define the terms, functions very differently from most marriage counselors. The former are active, directive, and see themselves as coaches, teachers, models. They give homework assignments to their clients, and accept the responsibility of showing them when and where they go wrong.

Finding A Good Marriage Counselor/ Trainer/Therapist

How do most people choose a therapist? Usually, through the recommendations of a friend, doctor, neighbor, colleague, or the Yellow Pages. The majority of practitioners are trained in a particular type of therapy, and in general you will get what that person knows, which may not necessarily be what is best for you or your marriage. Do not hesitate to see several therapists before choosing one. It is your happiness, time, money, and well-being that are at stake. So "shop around!" Decisions are not irrevocable. Don't feel obliged to stay with a therapist simply because you have been seeing him or her for months or years.

If the therapist (or his/her receptionist) is defensive and refuses to give you some free telephone time and straight answers, you have every right to be suspicious. When a professional has money-making as a major incentive and will not take five or six minutes to provide basic details, you will know in advance what to expect. Recently, a marriage counselor (whom I do *not* hold in high regard) mentioned that someone called his office and "had the gall" to expect him to disclose what treatment methods he employed. I asked: "What's wrong with that?" and added, "I think people have a right to know." He replied that he, as a professional, should not be questioned by a layperson. I consider that an unfortunate attitude that can only leave his clients feeling one-down.

If you are already receiving professional help, here are some basic questions you can answer yourself to ensure that your counselor/therapist is right for you:

- Do you feel comfortable with the therapist as a person?

- Does the therapist answer your questions directly rather than simply asking you what you think?

- Is the therapist willing to reveal things about himself or herself, either spontaneously or in response to your inquiries?

- Does the therapist encourage differences of opinion rather than insisting the you are "resisting" if you disagree with him or her?

- Do the therapist's comments and suggestions make sense to you?

A "No" to any of these questions suggests that there may be problems with the therapy. If you answered "No" to two or more of these questions, I would suggest that you find another therapist.

Conclusion

The well-known psychiatrist Carl Whitaker has pointed out that a bad marriage produces "hateful demons out of perfectly nice people."

In reviewing the many hundreds of couples I have treated since obtaining a license to do so in 1960, I am struck by the fact that three forces stand out as most responsible for marital unhappiness — *power*, *control*, and *ownership*. Negative consequences are bound to result when one spouse fails to perceive the other as a separate person with rights and privileges, a unique individual with a destiny of his or her own. To expect a spouse to do one's bidding and live up to predetermined expectations will create little more than mutual misery.

How far can one go with self-help? Surprisingly far, but clearly, when people have significant skill deficits (e.g., when they do not know how to be assertive and up-front), when they suffer from low self-esteem, severe depression, extreme anxiety, deep-seated guilt, or intense rage, professional help is necessary.

I recently concluded work with a couple I had been treating for almost two years. Both husband and wife needed antidepressant medication (for which a skillful psychiatrist was called in as a consultant) before I could even begin making headway with their other problems. It was necessary to change the way they reacted, not only to one another, but to all the significant people in their lives (their respective parents, siblings, employers, and associates). The manner in which they expressed their emotions was reminiscent of 12-year old children. Sexually, they were unenlightened and misinformed. Both suffered from low self-esteem and poor self-images. The erroneous and irrational ideas to which they subscribed took many months of reeducation. (Initially, they clung to Myths 5, 7, 8, 12,13, and 14.)

While a book such as this would have been quite useless in such an extreme case, fortunately most people are not nearly as distressed. I persisted with this difficult relationship because it was clear to me from the start that (a) this couple could be helped, (b) neither one would be better off without the other, and therefore (c) this marriage was worth saving.

Many marriages can be improved and, unless love is dead (Myth 18) or an extreme degree of basic incompatibility prevails, there are good grounds for optimism and hope. The first step, as I see it, is to discard each of the myths described in this book!

A Final Note

All good marriages are based on compromise. In a happy, successful marriage, people *share* each other's lives; they don't *run* each other's lives. Above all, please realize that marriage is not a romantic interlude; it is a practical and serious relationship. And a genuinely good marriage is more than precious — it is a joy to behold.

MY TOP EIGHT TIPS
FOR A GOOD RELATIONSHIP

1) Keep Criticism to a Bare Minimum

If there is something your partner does that displeases you, instead of coming on critically, ask him or her to act differently in future. Thus, "You looked like a fool when you told Sally in front of Sam and Meg that she ought to divorce George," would be changed to, "In future, I think it would be better if you made personal comments to Sally, or to anyone else, in private."

2) Avoid Saying "No"

Try to say "Yes" whenever feasible. Those who live on automatic "No!" create bitterness and resentment. Spouses want to feel loved, accepted and appreciated. Saying No to reasonable requests is highly toxic. If you are unable to say Yes, explain the situation fully. "I can't be at your sister's place before 6 PM because my boss wants us all to attend the stock option meeting from 5 to 7."

3) Show Appreciation

Relationships have to be nurtured. Expressions of appreciation and praise are necessary to keep a marriage on track. Too many people remain silent when things are going well, but the moment something is not to their liking, they criticize, and complain. Positive reinforcement is as important to a marriage as oil and gasoline are to a car.

4) Do Not Give Gratuitous Advice

Most people are irritated and feel resentful when given free advice that they never requested. If you are asked to express your opinion, it is fine to say what you believe your spouse should feel, think, or do. If not, you could inquire if he or she would like to hear your views on the matter. If the answer is "No thank you," drop it!

5) Don't Be a Mind Reader

It is a serious mistake to tell someone what he or she is thinking or feeling. Tom: "You believe your brother looks down on you." Sue:

(continues on next page)

"Where do you get that from? It's simply untrue." Tom: "You can't fool me." This type of exchange spells trouble. It is better to inquire, "Am I correct that you think your brother looks down on you?" And then accept the other person's answer — unless you can cite clear evidence to the contrary.

6) Don't Dredge Up the Past
If you hang onto negative experiences from the past and use them as battering rams, you are asking for trouble. Few things create distance and fuel resentment more than reminding someone about mistakes he has made, or unfortunate things she has said or done. The past is dead. Drop it! But do hang onto pleasant memories and events.

7) Don't Be a Control Freak
There may be people who enjoy being controlled by someone, living right under their thumb, but they are certainly in the minority. Control freaks must always be in command. They take charge and issue rules, regulations, decrees, orders, mandates, instructions, and demands. When two control freaks marry each other, the fur really flies. Constantly telling someone what and what not to do is the height of arrogance. There is usually a steep price to pay for it.

8) Do Not Reward Unkindness
Many people mistakenly believe that if they are kind and pleasant to someone who is mean and nasty, the net result will be greater generosity and beneficence from the perpetrator. Quite the contrary! If one behaves kindly in response to nastiness, one is only rewarding the very behavior that needs to be extinguished. Kindness will only encourage the person to continue being bad tempered. Why would he or she change? But if one is friendly, sympathetic, and good-hearted only in response to similar behaviors from others, chances are that the disagreeableness will diminish.

(I strongly recommend the book *Making It As A Couple* by Allen Fay, M.D., which lists 54 traps that undermine relationships. The book was published in 1998 by FMC books in Essex, Connecticut.)

Please see the following page for more books.